THEY NEVER ASKED

てのひらをたいやうにすかしてみる

They Never Asked

SENRYŪ POETRY FROM THE WWII
PORTLAND ASSEMBLY CENTER

Edited and translated by

SHELLEY BAKER-GARD

MICHAEL FREILING

SATSUKI TAKIKAWA

Foreword by DUANE WATARI

Oregon State University Press   Corvallis

Oregon State University Press in Corvallis, Oregon, is located within the traditional homelands of the Mary's River or Ampinefu Band of Kalapuya. Following the Willamette Valley Treaty of 1855, Kalapuya people were forcibly removed to reservations in Western Oregon. Today, living descendants of these people are a part of the Confederated Tribes of Grand Ronde Community of Oregon (grandronde.org) and the Confederated Tribes of the Siletz Indians (ctsi.nsn.us).

Cataloging-in-publication data is available from the Library of Congress. LCCN: 2023008517

ISBN 978-0-87071-235-7 paperback; ISBN 978-0-87071-236-4 ebook

∞This paper meets the requirements of ANSI/NISO Z39.48-1992 (Permanence of Paper).

First published in 2023 by Oregon State University Press

Printed in the United States of America

 **Oregon State University**
OSU Press

Oregon State University Press
121 The Valley Library
Corvallis OR 97331-4501
541-737-3166 • fax 541-737-3170
www.osupress.oregonstate.edu

This anthology is dedicated to those people who acknowledge the unlawfulness of the incarceration of the Japanese Americans during World War II and to those people who raise the red flags of protest against the oppression of the disadvantaged everywhere.

Contents

Foreword

DUANE WATARI

My grandfather, Masaki "Joe" Kinoshita, was a prolific writer. Starting around 1938, he began writing Japanese poetry (senryū). His pen name was Jōnan, which means "south of the castle" (when he lived in Japan, his home was literally south of the castle located in his prefecture). As was typical for a new senryū poet, a mentor or Sensei would work with an individual in getting started. Mr. Roy Yokota was that person who came to the house in the evenings to work with my grandfather. After working long hours and days in his family business, my grandfather still managed to fit in writing in his personal journals daily.

After World War II broke out in 1941, my grandfather and family were forced to move from their home, along with other Japanese Americans, to the WCCA Assembly Center in Portland, Oregon, in 1942. They were subsequently imprisoned at the Minidoka concentration camp in Idaho. In 1942, while at the camp, my grandfather joined the Portland Bara Ginsha Senryū group. Mr. Yokota was also there. They both continued to write poetry during and after incarceration. My family returned to Portland after the war ended and resumed the family business at the same location until retiring in 1979. During their absence, a neighbor friend had watched over their property as well as possible. Both the business store and the attached house were vandalized extensively during the war years.

In 1985, Pacific Northwest senryū poetry groups held a seventy-fifth anniversary celebration to honor the Hokubei Senryū Ginsha, which started in 1910 in Yakima, Washington (I'm not sure when Bara Ginsha started). On a personal note, I would like to recognize Ms. Hisako Saito, who was also a longtime member of Bara Ginsha and a very good friend of my grandfather until he passed away in 1996. Both have poems engraved in stone at the Japanese American Historical Plaza in Portland.

My grandfather wrote thousands of poems during his fifty-eight years as a poet. I have several boxes of his and other poems he liked. He dated the journals he used to record his poems, and this is where I found those from the years he was incarcerated during World War II. The boxes also contained personal diaries written for much of his life. I discovered

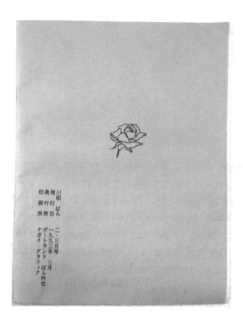

川柳
ばら

発行日　一九七三年　三月

発行所　ポートランド　ばら吟社

印刷所　ナガイ・グランド・グラフィク

二・三四号

Cover of a Bara Ginsha newsletter,
date unknown. Duane Watari
collection; photo credit: Shelley
Baker-Gard

these journals after going through our family keepsakes in my mother's
household belongings in preparation for selling her house. I felt the
poetry in particular had historical importance and needed to be shared.

In 2017, I began a search for Japanese poetry organizations in
Portland. There weren't any for senryū, but haiku poetry came up. The
Haiku Society of America (HSA) referred me to their local Portland
chapter, and HSA Oregon coordinator Shelley Baker-Gard. Shelley was
very interested; she felt my grandfather's poetry needed to be shared, as
it provided a piece of little-known history and insight through poetry
into the lives of Japanese Americans and their personal feelings while
imprisoned during World War II. The poems are all written in Japanese
kanji, and unfortunately my family could not translate them.

I'm a third-generation Japanese American, and the need to find out
what my family went through before, during, and after the war was of
special importance to me. Not enough has been said or written about
the Japanese pioneers as immigrants to the United States. My family did
not share their hardships; they instead chose to forget and move on. My
grandfather and others expressed their feelings in poetry, and for this we
are grateful they can now be understood.

Acknowledgments

Nothing is created by anyone without the knowledge and support, directly and indirectly, of many people. That statement is certainly true for the production of this anthology of World War II senryū, written in the spring of 1942 by Japanese American poets while they were held captive at the Wartime Civilian Control Administration (WCCA) Assembly Center in Portland, Oregon. These senryū were written in Japanese, and many thanks go to the translators and translation cultural advisers who helped with the literal translation to English. The editors of this anthology express their appreciation to the following cultural and translation advisers for their assistance with our project.

RINKO JEFFERS, an Issei who was born in Japan before World War II and is a US citizen currently living on Maui, Hawai'i. Jeffers leads an international haiku writing group, Haiku in English Maui (HIEM), and a Japanese-language haiku group, Maui Hototogisu-Kai. She has received numerous awards, including one from the Japanese Cultural Society of Maui for her efforts to promote intercultural understanding through the writing of haiku. She was honored in December of 2021 by the Japan Hototogisu School of Haiku when she was promoted to Dojin status. This is the first time in the school's 150 years history a Dojin has been appointed who is not residing in Japan.

AKIKO ANDERSON is bicultural and bilingual in Japanese. Mrs. Anderson provided many suggestions on the translations and interpretations of the poems. She is knowledgeable about Japanese poetry forms and composes poetry in Japanese as a member of the Japanese American Oregon Haiku Club established in 2001.

TERUKO KUMEI previously taught at the Shirayuri University in Chofu, Japan, and is the scholar who has completed perhaps the most extensive research on and translation of senryū written by Japanese Americans. Kumei's essays and articles on the Japanese senryū poets in the United States were invaluable for the cultural and historical information on the senryū genre. In addition, her help with the identification of the actual names of the poets, from their Japanese *gagō* (pen name), enabled us to provide biographical notes on the poets.

Former Oregon poet laureate **LAWSON FUSAO INADA** read the entire draft manuscript and provided many helpful suggestions. Particularly helpful for our research was his book, *Only What We Could Carry: The Japanese Internment Experience,* and his poetry collection *Legends from the Camp.*

SYLVIA GRAY, an Asian history professor at Portland Community College, who studied Japanese in Japan, donated many hours to reviewing the manuscript and also offered multiple suggestions regarding translations and editing.

Appreciation of the Oregon Historical Society (OHS) and the staff also needs to be mentioned. The OHS houses the complete collection of the WCCA Assembly Center's newsletter, *The Evacuazette.* The newsletter was published twice weekly during the three-month period the Japanese Americans were at the Portland WCCA Assembly Center in 1942.

Finally, gratitude and acknowledgment are extended to the many authors who have written about the incredible injustices levied on the Japanese American community during the World War II years. In particular, the concentration camp haiku anthology collected by Violet Kazue de Cristoforo, *May Sky: There Is Always Tomorrow,* was one of the most important sources of information, as was the book by Mitsuye Yamada, *Camp Notes and Other Writings.* Mitsuye Yamada also provided us with information about her father's senryū club in the Seattle area during the war.

Without the help of the people and organizations acknowledged above, this anthology would have been lacking in many aspects that provide additional insights into the incarceration of Japanese Americans.

Shelley Baker-Gard

In addition to the people and organizations mentioned above, I would like to express my personal appreciation to those who helped me understand the nature of the incarceration and its impact on the Japanese American community and who gave me my first exposure to Japan.

The late William Morlock, my high school teacher, first brought this tragedy to my attention in an unforgettable, albeit somewhat contentious, class one day. I nearly jumped out of my seat to challenge him. "This couldn't possibly have happened. If it had, I would have heard about it before now." To which Mr. Morlock wisely responded, "Go home and ask your father." I did, and the result was another explosive scene in the house.

Also, I want to thank two college buddies, Paul Nishijima and John Nishimoto, who now reside in Honolulu, Hawai'i. They were my first instructors in Japanese literature, and Japanese culture in general, as we read the novels of Kawabata and Mishima together, discussing them in late night "seminars." We are still in touch.

Finally, I would like to thank the Henry Luce Foundation for making possible my first visit to Japan as a Luce Scholar, in 1977, and for funding my initial instruction in the Japanese language, as well as the late Professor Makoto Nagao, for his kindness in hosting me at his Kyoto University laboratory that year.

Mike Freiling

Notes on Terminology

Throughout this manuscript, the editors have worked to use terminology that accurately reflects the actual experience and feelings of the Japanese American citizens who were unjustly incarcerated during World War II. Consequently, we have avoided usage of official government euphemisms, such as "internment," "evacuation," or "relocation," except in the quotation of other works.

Instead, we have chosen words that we believe are consistent with the recommendations offered by Densho and the Japanese American Museum of Oregon (JAMO) and also as detailed in Roger Daniel's article "Words Do Matter: A Note on Inappropriate Terminology and the Incarceration of the Japanese Americans." A manuscript of the length of this anthology typically requires use of more than one word for key elements, to avoid tedious repetition, and some readers will no doubt find some of the words we use more accurate than others. But as Neil Nakadate notes in *Looking after Minidoka: An American Memoir,* "any of the more recently advocated terms is preferable to 'relocation centers,' the U.S. government's euphemistic label in 1942."[1]

In considering these issues, we ask the reader to keep in mind that the true focus of our work is to celebrate the deep human characteristics of those who were incarcerated, particularly their endurance, resilience, and willingness to maintain hope amid conditions that were intolerable. We all have something to learn from their inspiring response to the injustices that were inflicted on them, even as we contemplate in shame the cruelty with which some Americans, and the government itself, chose to treat other citizens of their own country.

Introduction

The Beginning

Many historical projects have an interesting beginning, and this one is no exception. In late 2017, the Haiku Society of America provided my contact information to Duane Watari, because I was the HSA Oregon coordinator. He emailed me about the poetry notebooks of his grandfather, Masaki Kinoshita, in November while I was in Japan, and we agreed to meet after the holidays.

The poetry genre in which Mr. Watari's grandfather Masaki Kinoshita wrote was Japanese senryū. Senryū are similar to haiku in brevity but are generally about human relationships and/or interactions with humans, whereas haiku are generally about human relationships or interactions with the nonhuman world (Mother Nature, seasons, animals, and so on). In Japanese, both haiku and senryū have a rhythm that very often takes a 5-7-5 individual sound unit form (each unit is frequently referred to as an *on*, and there can be multiple *on* in a Japanese word). All the senryū in this anthology follow the 5-7-5 Japanese form. In Japanese words, the *on* sound is usually not as long as the English syllable.*

Masaki (Joe) Kinoshita was a well-known leader in the Japanese American community and a longtime Portland, Oregon, resident. Duane and I corresponded for a couple of months about the notebooks, which were all meticulously written in Japanese. Duane's mother, Mrs. Watari, had been storing the notebooks since his grandfather's death, and the family was looking for a home for them. I promised him I would look for a translator to see if we could have some of the poems translated into English. I put out a few inquiries among my fellow HSA members, and I received a couple of responses, but the complexity of the translation made it slow going.

Then, serendipitously, and with a tease of an unknown power, Michael Freiling came to the Portland Haiku Group meeting on February 9, 2018. When Mike introduced himself, he mentioned that he had

---

* See the essay "American English Senryū and Haiku" on page 137 for more detailed information on the differences between haiku and senryū written in the Japanese language and those written in English.

a doctorate degree, lived part-time in Kyoto, Japan, and knew Japanese (both spoken and written). During our meeting break, I quickly cornered him, told him our story, and asked for his help. I was incredibly happy to hear his response—that he was willing to help—but it would be a couple of months before we could meet, as he was returning to Japan.

I let Duane know about Mike Freiling and his willingness to attempt the translations of some of the poetry. Duane and I finally met in person in March 2018. At that meeting, he gave me a look at a few of the many notebooks. One immediately stood out; it had a handwritten title in English and Japanese: *W.C.C.A. Assembly Center 1942 – North Portland, ORE. NO.2* (the cover of this book has a picture of part of that journal cover). When I picked it up and felt its smooth worn cover, I had an overwhelming sense of the passage of time, which took me back to this period of history, where tragedies were levied on the Japanese Issei (the first immigrant generation) and Nisei (the children of the Issei) living in the United States during World War II. The Portland WCCA Assembly Center was located in north Portland and was formerly the Pacific International Livestock Exposition Center (currently referred to as the Portland Expo Center, at 2060 N Marine Drive). This assembly center, like others along the west coast, was a stockyard that had previously housed horses. As a result of President Roosevelt's Executive Order No. 9066, the horse stalls were converted into tiny living spaces to house Japanese Americans and their families who had been forced to leave their homes and businesses.

At the March meeting, Duane and I talked about his grandfather, Masaki Kinoshita, who was known as Joe Kinoshita to many people in Portland and was born in Japan in 1896. He signed his senryū with the *gagō*, or pen name, Jōnan, which means "south of the castle." Kinoshita was also a member of the Bara Ginsha (Rose City) group until his death at age ninety-nine, in 1997. Both Duane and I felt that this particular WCCA journal was of historical significance. We agreed that we should focus on it for the translation of his grandfather's senryū and the senryū of several other poets.

In April 2018, Mike Freiling, Duane Watari, and I met to discuss the project and the journal. After that meeting, Mike and I agreed that Mike would do the literal translations of the Japanese, and I would then do a "free translation" of the literal and put the poem in an English senryū form. Often the literal translation was very close to an English form and was used. Mike enlisted the help of Satsuki Takikawa, a Japanese citizen and English teacher in Kyoto, Japan. Satsuki quickly became

表紙の次のページの裏の詩が、上下逆に印刷されてしまい
ました。又、この詩の8番目の漢字に誤りがありました。
　　（向）という字は 誤りです。
　　正しくは(間)です (p.120　#67 の詩)。
読者の皆様及び関係者の皆様に、ご迷惑をおかけしました
ことを深くお詫び申し上げます。

The poem on the page immediately following the initial title page
was inadvertently copied from a very early draft. The poem is printed
upside down, and the eighth character in the poem is incorrect. The
correct poem can be found on page 120 (poem #67).

The front of the first WCCA journal (May–June 1942), which was discovered after translations from the no. 2 journal were completed.

a cotranslator and coeditor for this project. We also enlisted the help of Rinko Jeffers, a Nisei Japanese American fluent in Japanese and the leader of two haiku groups on Maui, Hawai'i. Akiko Anderson, who lives in the Portland area, provided additional help with the translation.

The collection of senryū in this anthology was all found in the second journal written by the group of poets at the North Portland WCCA Assembly Center. At the beginning of this project, we did not know what had happened to the first journal, which would have been written in the first months of the center's opening. We speculated that it may have been confiscated, as writing in Japanese was frequently forbidden by the US military at the centers and camps. However, toward the end of this project, Duane Watari did find the first WCCA journal in storage. It contains senryū written from May to July. Another senryū journal of Masaki Kinoshita's was written at Minidoka, but it has not been translated into English. Its cover is pictured on page 121.

The journal used for this anthology contains approximately 450 senryū, written and recorded during a two-week period between August 8 and August 22, 1942. As many as twenty-two senryū poets participated at each of the WCCA senryū club meetings. During these two weeks, they met a total of four times and produced more than one hundred senryū per meeting. The meeting format at the assembly center is not known, but generally at these meetings the participants are provided one

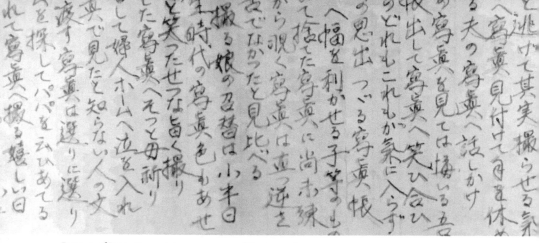

Picture of Japanese script on one page of the journal.

or more topics for their poem, then, at the meeting (or possibly before the meeting), they write the senryū and submit it to a leader, who either chooses which one is the best of all the submissions or asks the participants to vote on which is the best before the poets' names are revealed. Often the senryū are read aloud by the poet to the group. In this journal, each of the senryū was recorded by Masaki Kinoshita with the pen name of the poet.

At the August 8 meeting, the topics chosen were Connections, Talking About Anything and Sensibility and Discretion; at the August 15 meeting, the topics were Habits and About Anything; at the August 16 meeting, the one topic was Resolution/Readiness; at the August 22 meeting, the topics were About Anything, Confusion, and Doubt. The journal ends one week before the center residents began leaving on August 29, 1942, by train and bus, in groups of five hundred people, to incarceration camps.

Many of the Japanese Americans from the state of Washington who initially were at the North Portland Assembly Center were sent to the Heart Mountain camp in Wyoming. Those predominantly from Oregon left in early September and were taken to the Minidoka camp in Idaho. Some of the poets were also incarcerated in the Tule Lake camp in Northern California.

The environment at the Tule Lake camp was more restrictive, as Tule Lake was where the military also sent Japanese Americans who were wrongly suspected of disloyalty. Despite their harsh living conditions, the Japanese Americans poets did not stop writing poetry, and there are published collections of haiku poetry from multiple camps. But as of yet, no other anthology of World War II senryū has been published. Both of

Masaki Kinoshita's World War II journals have now been digitized by the Denshō organization in Seattle, Washington.

The work on the translation and research continued after our April 2018 meeting, and we met periodically to discuss the translations and progress. At one of our meetings, I brought several reference books to share (see bibliography). One of them was the autobiography *Nisei Daughter,* by Monica Sone, whose birth name was Kazuko Ito. She was born in Seattle, Washington, in 1919. Prior to World War II, in 1938, Sone was a patient at the Firland Sanitorium in Washington; while there, she and Betty Macdonald became friends. MacDonald wrote *The Plague and I,* in which she described their friendship and mutual struggle with tuberculosis. During World War II, more than two hundred Japanese Americans came down with tuberculosis and died while incarcerated.[1]

In *Nisei Daughter,* Sone relates how the family had to prepare themselves for the visits from the FBI at the beginning of World War II. Her mother, who was a tanka poet (tanka, also known as *waka,* is another short form of Japanese poetry, usually with a Japanese *on* line count of 5-7-5-7-7), was upset that she had to leave behind her *Man'yōshū,* because it was written in Japanese and therefore would raise suspicion with the FBI (the *Man'yōshū* is an anthology of Japanese poetry written between the fourth and eighth centuries and compiled in the eighth century). As

Japanese Americans from Washington boarding a bus for the Heart Mountain camp. Photo credit: Oregon Historical Society Archives (ID#: PF584-C_202204)

I related this story to Duane and Mike, Duane coincidently mentioned his family knew Monica Sone's family. Monica's mother Benko Ito continued to write tanka when they were incarcerated at Minidoka in 1942. Masaki Kinoshita and his family were also at Minidoka during this time.

In the fall of 2019, Mike Freiling completed the initial literal translation of the senryū and began adding the Japanese script to include with the English translations. We also decided to add another twelve senryū to the anthology. At this meeting, I decided we needed to have more background information relating to the events that were happening in the assembly center. For example, I believed the senryū relating to the birth of a baby at the center would have a historical record. Senryū, by definition, are a result of a poet's experience with events in human lives and are embedded in the context of the poet's life. As Ian Barker posits, "Context is everything," and "we must ground our work in a rich understanding of the context of use, or else we run the risk of creating well-meaning rubbish."[2]

After this meeting, I went to the Oregon Historical Society and copied every issue of the *Evacuazette*, the assembly center's newsletter, written by Nisei volunteers living at the center. The newsletter proved to be an invaluable source for information on the physical and social environments wherein the senryū were written. As a result of this research, many of the senryū in the anthology have a contextual note added to aid in correctly understanding the original meaning intended by the poet.

Life in the North Portland Assembly Center

Executive Order No. 9066, signed by President Franklin Roosevelt on February 19, 1942, enabled the US Army Wartime Civil Control Administration (WCCA) to incarcerate 3,676 Japanese Americans at the Portland International Livestock Exposition Center (currently referred to as the Expo Center, at 2060 N Marine Drive). The WCCA hastily converted animal stalls into tiny apartments for the families forced to leave their homes throughout Oregon and in the Yakima Valley, Washington, area. Families were required to report to the North Portland Assembly Center by May 5, 1942, and were allowed to take from their homes only what they could carry with them. Many lost whatever they left behind, and or had to sell their possessions below their market value. The center was occupied from May 2 to September 10, 1942, while the construction of more permanent incarceration camps in Idaho (Minidoka), Wyoming (Heart Mountain), and Northern California (Tule Lake) was under way.[3]

Diagram of the Portland Assembly Center interior, image from June 1942 Evacuazette assembly center newsletter. Oregon Historical Center files

Perhaps the best description of what life was like in the assembly center was provided by Minoru Yasui. In 1942, Yasui was a Portland attorney. On the night of March 28, 1942, he purposely and bravely broke the curfew mandate imposed on American citizens of Japanese descent. His subsequent arrest allowed him to file a lawsuit challenging the constitutional legitimacy of the curfew law (the Supreme Court did not rule in his favor). While waiting for the results of the lawsuit, Yasui was at the Portland WCCA Assembly Center. When he was there, he became active in the Nisei forum as an adviser on the governance of the center.[4] In September, he departed with other Oregon Japanese Americans when they were transferred to the Minidoka incarceration camp. Yasui was removed from Minidoka in November 1942 to serve his sentence of nine months in solitary confinement at the Multnomah County Jail (his time at Minidoka rightly counted toward the twelve-month prison sentence). In August of 1943, he was returned to Minidoka until June of 1944, when he received a release for employment in Chicago, Illinois.[5]

Decades later, on July 16, 1981, Minoru Yasui provided testimony on behalf of the National Committee for Redress and the Japanese American Citizens League. The testimony was presented to the Commission on Wartime Relocation and Internment of Civilians and describes well the environment of the assembly center life:[6]

I can testify from personal experience and observation that the North Portland WCCA assembly center was a livestock exposition hall, surrounded by man proof fences, topped with concertinas of barbed wire, and with guard towers equipped with searchlights at strategic intervals. Within the vast rambling building, where animals had been quartered, the footing underneath was asphalt; the stalls where animals had been stabled, the walls were calcimined. inasmuch as the quarters were intended to be only temporary, some mangers were still in place—and many a baby of Japanese ancestry—deemed by the Commanding General to pose a potential threat to the security of the United States—slept in such mangers at the North Portland livestock pavilion, which reminds of another babe who similarly slept in a manger some 2,000 years ago, only to grow up to be crucified. Certainly, substantial numbers of the evacuee population were devout Christians, and this humbling parallel was not lost on them.

Although it is true that full disclosures of the unspeakable activities being carried on in the Nazi concentration camps in Europe were not fully known, as of 1942, nevertheless enough was known of large contingents of Jews who were being shipped to various destinations in the Greater Reich like cattle—and speculation was rife, Unthinkable atrocities were suspected, and the consequences of the Nazi policies were blood-chilling. Surely those kinds of things could not happen in America! But, in the North Portland livestock barn, in 1942, where some 4,000 human beings were confined like cattle, there were scary rumors, apprehensions and fears in regard to frightening similarities, especially as large headlines in local newspapers clamored: "MAKE THE JAPS SUFFER!", "LET THEM HURT AND BE MISERABLE!", "CASTRATE 'EM, STERILIZE 'EM", "SHIP THEM OUT!", "GET RID OF THEM!"

The uncertainty, the not knowing what was going to happen, not knowing where we would be shipped or what would be there when we got there, not knowing when mass movements would take place, not knowing for how long we would be confined, or indeed not knowing whether any of us would get out alive—all of these unknowns posed tremendous anxieties on individuals, and especially on those with families.

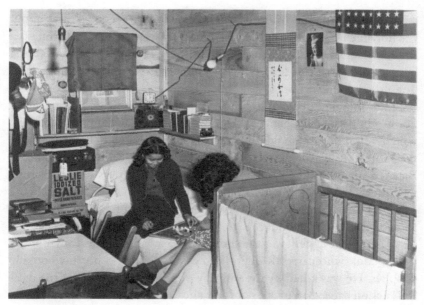

Living quarters for one family inside the assembly center. Photo credit: Oregon Historical Society

We were confined in the North Portland livestock barn for four, hot and stifling months, from May through June, July, and August 1942. In the crowded and congested confines of that livestock barn, life somehow went on; we were not permitted outdoors, except those who were ill of infectious disease, and as to those an infirmary was constructed at the rear of the main building. We survived; somehow the days and nights went by in dull, monotonous procession. The food was terrible, but nutritious and served in huge quantities; people got stomach upsets from the strong soap residue left on cooking utensils and on plates, cups and dishes. The living quarters were primitive, and the continuous noise of people talking, or coughing or sneezing, or someone having a bad dream at night, was nerve wracking. During the day, there were interminable card games, and for young folks, nursery schools, crafts, dancing, and other social activities which the evacuees operated and conducted. But time in confinement dragged through that hot, hot summer.

Not included in Minoru Yasui's testimony were the stories about the horrible infestation of flies that continually swarmed and tormented the imprisoned. These stories of life in the assembly center have often been passed down to the younger generations of Japanese Americans. The fly invasion was brought about when the center's fire department, on a hot July day, decided to cool things off by hosing down the center floors. Unfortunately, beneath the plywood floor lay manure-laced dirt, which, upon becoming wet, created a horrible stench that attracted the flies. The *Evacuazette* newsletter reported that the center manager, Mr. Bican, declared war on the flies and ordered fly swatters for each family in addition to five thousand flypaper strips and pesticide spraying. In the July 31 *Evacuazette*, the staff reported an estimate of 1,700,000 flies on those strips hanging about the center.[7]

Another incident was the shooting of a Japanese American military police cook who came through the entrance gates to borrow cooking supplies. He was killed by the military police in the middle of the day.[8] This action caused an increase of fear and anxiety in all the families who were already wondering what their fate was to be at the hands of the military. The incident was censored from the *Evacuazette* reporting.

Leaving the Center

One of the few ways individuals and families could leave the Portland WCCA Assembly Center was to volunteer to work in the beet fields in Malheur County. The Utah-Idaho Sugar Company and the Amalgamated Sugar Company, which owned a sugar processing plant in Nyssa, Idaho, needed field hands, and they convinced President Franklin D. Roosevelt to make an exception for the incarcerated Japanese Americans. As a result, in May 1942, several hundred families moved into a camp, formerly run by the New Deal Farm Security Administration, near Nyssa. The *Evacuazette* printed several articles on volunteers at the beet fields. Many of these Japanese Americans stayed in the area after the war and established new homes.[9]

Also, in May 1942, the National Japanese American Student Relocation Council was formed by the American Friends Service Committee to coordinate the release of college students to eastern and midwestern universities and colleges. Many of the students had been previously enrolled in Oregon colleges when they were incarcerated at the WCCA center in Portland. Approximately four thousand students in the exclusion zone were able to leave their imprisonment thanks to this program; however, many felt obligated to stay with their Issei parents to act as

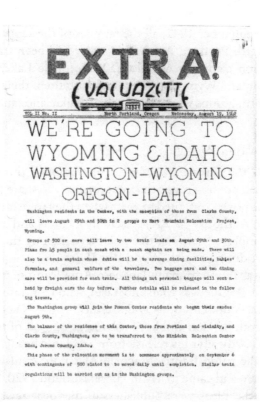

Front page of the final edition of the Evacuazette newsletter of the Portland Assembly Center. https://www.oregonhistoryproject.org/articles/historical-records/we39re-going-to-wyoming-amp-idaho/#.YulyXezMKWY

interpreters at the camps.[10] A few other Japanese Americans were also released for employment if they had obtained employment in the states not affected by the forced removal of Japanese Americans.

The Nisei were additionally able to leave their imprisonment in another way. Starting in the spring of 1942, United States Army recruiters came to the assembly centers and camps in hopes of enlisting young Japanese American Nisei to defend the United States. The Nisei were patriotic citizens, and many did enlist, even while their families remained behind barbed wire fences. They became part of the 100th/442nd Regimental Combat Team, which became the most decorated unit of World War II. In 2011, President Obama awarded the entire 100th Regimental Combat Team the Congressional Gold Medal. Many of the Nisei lives ended in battle, and many senryū reflect the effects their deaths had on their Issei parents.[11]

By early September 1942, all the families of the senryū and haiku poets at the North Portland Assembly Center had been transferred to the concentration camps in Minidoka, Idaho; Tule Lake, California; and Heart Mountain, Wyoming. They took with them their poetry, and continued to form groups who wrote senryū, haiku, and tanka at each of these camps.

Other Incarceration Poetry

As mentioned, the Japanese American community throughout the United States had poetry groups that met regularly to share their poetry. Very often these poets continued to write when they were incarcerated at War Relocation Authority (WRA) Assembly Centers and camps. What follows are examples of some of this poetry, written by the poets or by family members during or after World War II.

Hawai'i was home to many Japanese American poets before and after World War II. One was Matsuno Yasui, who composed tanka that poignantly reflects the emotions and sacrifice of the Nisei enlistment. Matsuno lost both her son and her husband as a result of the war (her husband died shortly after his release from an illness brought on by the conditions of the camp imprisonment).* Matsuno Yasui was born in Hiroshima, Japan, and came to live in Hawai'i around 1920. She and her husband, Satosuke Yasui, were publishers of the local newspaper *Maui News* (*Maui Shimbun*).There she established a tanka group called Shinju (true wood). These World War II tanka, also known as *waka*, were originally published in her anthology, *Waka of Maui*. In 2021, Rinko Jeffers found Matsuno Yasui's anthology in an old bookstore and donated it to the Maui World War II Nisei Veteran's Memorial Center in Kahului, Maui. Jeffers also wrote an article about Matsuno Yasui's story, which was published in May 2021 by the Japanese poetry magazine *Hototogisu*. Two of Matsuno's tanka are shown here.

> to see his dad
> the visit denied
> my broken-hearted son
> off to the front
> and I must cheer

---

* The editors do not know if Matsuno Yasui was related to the Hood River, Oregon, Yasui family.

> I try hard but
> I tremble too much
> to touch the flag
> stars and stripes cover
> my son's casket

In 1983, several poets published an anthology of tanka poetry they had composed while incarcerated at various locations on the mainland United States. This anthology, *Poets Behind Barbed Wire*, was edited and translated by Jiro Nakano and Kay Nakano, with illustrations by George Hoshida.

The Issei poets featured in this anthology are Keiho Soga, Taisan-boku Mori, Sojin Takei, and Muin Ozaki. All were leaders in their communities when Pearl Harbor was bombed, and all were quickly arrested and incarcerated until after the war when they returned to Hawai'i. Below are two tanka from the collection.[12] The first is by Muin Ozaki, who was at several camps (this tanka was composed at Fort Sill, Oklahoma); his final imprisonment was at the Tule Lake camp in Northern California.

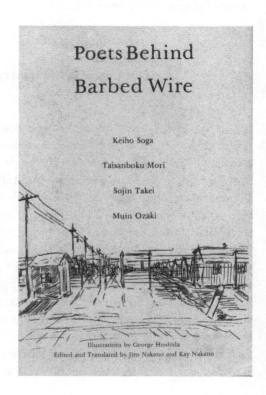

Cover of the Tanka chapbook
Poets Behind Barbed Wire.

a wrenching anguish rises
as the number "111"
is painted
on my naked chest
in red

The second tanka is by Sojin Takei, who founded the Maui Tanka Poetry Club with Satosuke Yasui (the husband of Matsuno Yasui). Takei was also at multiple camp locations, the last one at Crystal City, Texas. His tanka was written the night he was arrested.

while the MPs wait
you fill my suitcase
and spill your tears
how heavy its weight

While incarcerated at the Minidoka camp in Idaho, another tanka poet, Shizue Iwatsuki, from Hood River, Oregon, wrote the following tanka expressing similar sentiments:

three children sacrificed
to this alien land,
now the aged father hauls coal
through falling snow[13]

One of the most important and comprehensive anthologies of Japanese American World War II incarceration haiku was compiled, translated, and prefaced by Violet Kazue de Cristoforo (1917–2007) in *May Sky: There Is Always Tomorrow: An Anthology of Japanese American Concentration Camp Kaiko Haiku.* Kazue de Cristoforo was a remarkable woman. She was born in Hilo, Hawai'i, and attended school in both the United States and Japan. Prior to World War II she lived in Fresno, California, and married Shigeru Matsuda, who was a member of the Valley Ginsha Haiku Kai of Fresno. They had two children prior to the war. When the family was forced to leave their home in April 1941, they were incarcerated at the Fresno Assembly Center (a former stockyard); there, she gave birth in one-hundred-degree heat to their third child. After first being sent to the Jerome, Arkansas, camp, they were transferred to Tule Lake, California, where she and her husband were members of the Tule Lake Valley Ginsha. In 1944, her husband was repatriated to Japan.[14]

After the war, Violet and the children returned to Japan in 1946. There she found her parents had lost their home and suffered greatly because of the bombing of Japan. By this time, her husband had remarried, and she subsequently divorced him. In 1953, she married Wilfred H. de Cristoforo and returned to Monterey, California. For many decades, she advocated for redress legislation, including testifying before the congressional Commission on Wartime Relocation and Internment of Civilians in 1981. She also published six books, including a collection of her poems at Tule Lake, *Ino Hana: Poetic Reflections of Tule Lake Internment* (1987).[15] In 2007, Violet Kazue de Cristoforo was honored by the National Endowment for the Arts with a National Heritage Achievement award for her many publications about haiku in the Japanese American community.

In the *May Sky* anthology, de Cristoforo documents many of the haiku written by members of three Californian Japanese American haiku groups: the Delta Ginsha of Stockton, which was established in 1918; the Valley Ginsha Haiku Kai of Fresno, established in 1928; and the Tule Lake Valley Ginsha. The groups followed the practices of the free-form *kaiko* poets, who did not ascribe to the need for a 5-7-5 Japanese sound unit *on* pattern, nor did they require the inclusion of a Japanese *kigo* or season word. The following poems are from the anthology and were translated by de Cristoforo, who includes the original Japanese script with her "free renditions" of each haiku.[16]

The first example is by Yotenchi Agari, a member of the Delta Ginsha group. This haiku was written when his family was leaving for the Stockton Assembly Center.

Rhododendron blooms
about to leave my house
where my child was born[17]

The second haiku is by Hisao Fukuda, who was at the Rohwer camp in Arkansas. While there, he gathered potatoes with incarcerated Italian Americans:

Both sides laughing
not understanding the language
face wet with snow

The following haiku was written by Hyakuissei Okamoto when martial law was declared at Tule Lake and some of the Japanese Americans protesting it were arrested.

> Winter night
> pale faced man
> taps my shoulder

The above haiku are just a few of the approximately three hundred haiku that appear in de Cristoforo's anthology.

The Canadian government also incarcerated their Japanese immigrants and Japanese Canadian citizens. Canadian author and haiku poet Jaqueline Pearce is currently leading an effort to translate haiku written at the Tashme camp in British Columbia; the following haiku is from the collection. The poet used the pen name Konon (Lonely Village) and wrote the haiku after the tragic drowning of a child from the camp.[18]

> people panicking
> the emergency bell rises
> to the summer sky

Additionally, poets were imprisoned in US POW camps both in the United States and in Japan during the US occupation of Japan after

Tashme Internment Camp, British Columbia, Canada, 1942. Photo credit: University of British Columbia, Japanese Canadian Research Collection (ID#JCPC-30-013)

the war. Here is an example of one haiku by avant-garde haiku poet
Kaneko Tohta (1919–2018), who wrote this poem based on his own
experiences:

> the disappearing wake—
> leaving behind the scorched fire
> of unmarked graves [19]

Thousands of haiku, tanka, and senryū were written by Japanese
American poets during World War II. Some were published in small col-
lections and in Japanese American newspapers; however, most were not,
and many were lost or destroyed. All of the poetry takes one to the mo-
ment of time, place, and emotion being experienced by the poet—these
poems are micro-history stories to be relived by the reader.

A Brief History of Senryū and Haiku in Japanese American Community Origins

To understand the history of senryū and haiku in the Japanese American
community, a short synopsis of the history of haiku and senryū is neces-
sary. Both senryū and haiku are forms of Japanese poetry that are very dif-
ferent from traditional English-language poetry. They have no intended
rhyme, meter, or alliteration, but they do have a rhythmical resonance in
spoken Japanese, created by the vowel-consonant pattern in the Japanese
language.[20] Traditional Japanese senryū and haiku forms share the same
ancestral parent, in the form of the Japanese *renga*, a poem that is com-
posed with multiple linked verses, written collectively by multiple poets,
which frequently takes place in a group setting. Each *renga* stanza has
particular compositional and sequential rules: for instance, a verse with a
specified theme or subject, such as writing about the moon, has to occur
in a particular location of the *renga*. Another requirement is a seasonal
indicator (later referred to as a *kigo*, which is a specific season reference
word, such as "spring" or "cherry blossom," which are catalogued by the
Japanese in a codex called a *saijiki*). Each *renga* poet takes a turn writing
a stanza that must link to the prior stanza. In the fourteenth and fifteenth
centuries, *renga* became a widespread collaborative form of poetry (still
practiced in modern times throughout the world and in an evolved form
called *renku*).[21]

Collaborative linked verse became a popular form of entertain-
ment in Japan as early as 712 AD, as recorded in the Japanese document
called the *Kojiki* or *Furukotofumi* (Record of Ancient Matters), which is

a collection of Shinto myths and other writings believed to be the oldest Japanese literary work available in modern times.[22] Writing poetry at that time in Japanese history was primarily an aristocratic pastime.[23] Poems written in Japanese, as opposed to an adapted version of Chinese, were called *waka*. One of the most common forms of *waka*, known as tanka, had five segments (lines) and a 5-7-5-7-7 sound unit *on* pattern.

Poetry written in a linked verse form was included in the *Man'yōshū*, which included examples of dialogue poems, where one poet would write the 5-7-5 section and the other poet would finish it with the 7-7 section of the *waka* (this is now referred to as a *tan-renga* when composed with another poet). Rinko Jeffers explains: "In Japanese *Ka* (歌) means a song, a verse, a poem and *Wa* (和) means 'Japanese' *Wa-Ka* = Japanese poem; '*Tan* (短)' means 'short'—*Tan-Ka* = short poem."

Haiku

The seventeenth century ushered in a change in direction for Japanese poetry. An additional form was created from *renga*, called *haikai*. This form became popular with the working and merchant classes of Japan because it was frequently about everyday life and often was humorous.[24] *Haikai* developed into a style known as *haikai no renga* under the leadership of one of the most honored poets of Japan, Matsuo Bashō (1644–1694). This style focused on the introductory section of the *renga*, called the *hokku*, and had the 5-7-5 Japanese *on* count pattern. Bashō had many followers, and over the years of his teaching, he encouraged a sense of *kamu* or lightness and spirituality in the *hokku*. Bashō was a devout Zen Buddhist, steeped in Shinto cultural traditions, who saw the *hokku* as an intuitive expression of a human emotion linked to a connection with nature.[25]

In the late nineteenth century, another haiku master, Masaoka Shiki (1867–1902), was the first Japanese poet to use the term *haiku* instead of the term *hokku*, adding an emphasis to its detachment from the *renga* as a stand-alone poetry form.[26] Shiki held the belief that the language of haiku should be objective—a *shasei*, meaning a sketch of the moment or experience rather than a poem from the subjective imagination. However, he also believed that, with practice, an experienced haiku poet could create a haiku by taking this objective experience and reflecting from it a perceived ontological or personal truth.[27] Shiki's influence on the Japanese poets was extensive, and the term *haiku* replaced the term *hokku* for this short form of *waka*. Not until the early twentieth century was the influence of Shiki and his disciples (including his descendants who inherited Shiki's leadership) challenged by the New Rising Haiku movement.*

Some haiku poets in Japan, such as Kawahigashi Hekigotō (1873–1937), who was once a student of Masaoka Shiki, began to accept haiku form changes. These poets were at times persecuted for their proletarian viewpoints and for their nontraditional style of haiku.[28] Hekigotō suggested his new "free-style" poems not be referred to as haiku; instead, he preferred the term *tanshi* (literally meaning a short poem). This new style began around 1907 to 1915, when Hekigotō, with other poets including Ippekiro Nakatsuka,[29] developed haiku compositions that did not require either a *kigo* (a Japanese season word) or a strict 5-7-5 sound unit count. These new leaders were part of the New Rising Haiku movement, and the changed poetry became known as *gendai* (modern haiku). Hekigotō and Nakatsuka's poetry was also known as *kaiko* (free-form).

As mentioned, two Japanese American haiku groups, the Delta Ginsha of Stockton, California (established in 1918), and the Valley Ginsha of Fresno, California (established in 1928), followed the teachings of the free-form (*kaiko*) poets. Violet de Cristoforo described the style they ascribed to as one that "stimulated . . . a free, intuitive expression of one's state of mind. Love and observation of nature . . . and elegant usage of words were the focal points." The groups did not, as in the traditional Japanese haiku form, use *kigo* season words, which are culturally enriched and, like *renga*, also catalogued in the *saijiki*. However, their haiku nearly always contained a connection to nature.[30]

Not all Japanese Americans followed the free style of haiku. Instead, they continued to follow the traditional 5-7-5 *on* sound count and wrote with a *kigo* season word. They sometimes would have a *haijin*, or master haiku poet in Japan, to advise them and generally followed the views of Masaoka Shiki and his descendants.

Senryū

The evolution of senryū, like that of haiku, occurred in the mid-seventeenth century. While Matsuo Bashō was working to refine the *hokku* form, other seventeenth-century *renga* teachers continued on the path of earning their living by teaching collaborative *haikai* poetry that adhered to less spirituality and more humorous themes than Bashō's followers generally practiced. These short *haikai* poems placed more emphasis on

---

* See the essay "American English Senryū and Haiku" on p. XX for further discussion on the New Rising Haiku movement.

the everyday experiences of human-to-human relationships. The teachers commonly used a technique known as *maekuzuke* for instruction of the *haikai*. They started the *maekuzuke* by writing a segment of the *renga* called a *maeku*.[31] The *maeku* part of the *renga* was about fourteen *on* sound units long and set the theme for the next section of the *renga*. The *maeku* had themes similar to the seasonless *renga* verses following the *hokku* (for instance, a subject such as "love" would be a theme for a *maeku*).The students would respond to the *maeku* with a longer composition called the *tsukeku*, which was usually about seventeen to nineteen *on* sound units long.[32]

Toward the beginning of the eighteenth century, the *maekuzuke* further evolved into very popular contests. *Maekuzuke* master teachers (*tenja*) received hundreds of entries for the *tsukeku* response—each accompanied with an entry fee.[33] All the entries were signed with pen names, which allowed greater freedom in poking fun at or satirizing wealthy government officials and human life in general. For example, here is an example of a *tsukeku* (later called a *senryū*) about gender relations that we can easily understand today:

> "All women . . ."
> he begins, and then
> glances around[34]

The *tenja* was the judge of the contest and selected the winning entry. The poet who won received recognition and a prize. Eventually the short *maeku* portion of the contest was left off and the *tsukeku* became a stand-alone poem of a 5-7-5 sound unit construction, as it is in the *hokku*, but again with no reference needed to nature or seasons. The *tsukeku* became the direct ancestor to the senryū.

The form is called *senryū* (which means "river willow") because it was derived from the name of the *maekuzuke* poem master Karai Senryū (1718–1790). Over time, his skill at composing the beginning *maeku* stanza was widely recognized, and his contests became extremely popular and garnered him a large following of poets. His name became synonymous with the *tsukeku*, and the term *senryū* was used from the eighteenth century to current times to distinguish it from other *haikai*, *waka*, or *hokku* (during Karai Senryū's time, haiku were still called *hokku*). In 1765, Karai Senryū began publishing the winning *tsukeku* entries in an anthology called *The Willow Barrel* (*Yanagi-daru*—柳樽). The editor, Goryōken Arubeshi (?–1788), decided to publish them without the *maeku* because, like other *haikai norenga*, and like *hokku*, they could be understood as complete poems.[35] Arubeshi also wanted to elevate the *tsukeku* to the level of appreciation afforded to the *hokku* and other more serious *haikai*. The senryū form remained popular for many decades following Karai Senryū's death from spinal tuberculosis in 1790.

However, by the mid-nineteenth century, senryū had devolved (with some exceptions) into a much less evocative and inspired form, becoming a trite, pun-filled, and sometimes pornographic expression of human life. Senryū poetry during this period was scorned and became mixed in with other poetry forms at that time that were collectively called *kyōku* (mad poems, also called Ko-Senryū).[36]

Fortunately, in the early 1900s, senryū regained its reputation as a more serious form of commentary on the human condition and our relationships with each other. It became modernized when a senryū revitalization movement was initiated under the leadership of journalists Sakai Kuraki (1869–1945) and Inoue Kenkabo (1870–1934). Sakai Kuraki, who worked for the newspaper *Nippon*, wanted to see senryū return to the themes and style Karai Senryū had promoted in the seventeenth-century anthologies. Kuraki published his viewpoints in the book *The Outline of Senryū* and, in 1905, founded the senryū magazine *Satsukigoi (May Carp)*. Another journalist, Inoue Kenkabo, started a popular senryū column in the *Nippon*, called *Yanagidaru*, which encouraged poets to write on current affairs and topics discussed by the working and middle-class people of Japan. Kenkabo also founded the magazine *Senryū* in 1904.[37] By 1935, few Japanese newspapers did not have a senryū column in addition to a haiku column. This tradition continues in modern times, and Japanese papers include articles with haiku, senryū, and tanka.

Besides human foibles, the topics covered by the new senryū poets included antiwar sentiments, labor union issues, economic depression (after World War I), and other societal concerns. In 1910, arguing against keeping senryū, haiku, and tanka as separate genres, the editors of the magazine *Shin senryū (New Senryū)*, Anzai Ichian and Ando Genkaibō, thought that haiku, senryū, and other short poems were not particularly different from each other and should be categorized not as haiku or senryū but simply as short poetry.[38]

One example of a senryū published during this revival period is this one by Morita Katsuji (1892–1979), the leader of the leftist senryū poets that used senryū to promote socialism and communism in the 1920s.

a labor strike—
the chain is loosened
by a few inches[39]

It was the modernized senryū style that Japanese Americans adopted and brought with them when they immigrated to the United States at the beginning of the twentieth century. Many Japanese-language newspapers in the United States published the senryū in regular columns set aside specifically for senryū. The first senryū poetry circle in the United States was established in Yakima, Washington, sometime between 1910 and 1912, when a group of Japanese American workers gathered to share their senryū with each other. A record of the meeting shows that the winning senryū voted the best by the group was written by Kentsuku Kurokawa.[40] That senryū was

next morning,
all sobered up. damn.
sake brewed brawls.[41]

It is easy to understand this senryū, and Teruko Kumei sums up the meaning well by describing it as "a situation where an overindulgence in sake caused discord amongst friends and the likely need for apologies the next day."[42]

The Yakima group was called the Yakima Ameikai (Yakima Croaking Society). Kahō Honda (pen name Shinjiro) was their leader for two years until he took an extended trip to Japan. When he returned to Seattle, he formed another senryū group in 1929. This group was named Hokubei Senryū Gosenkai (Senryū Society of North America) and held weekly meetings.[43] Kahō Honda was one of the poets incarcerated at the Portland Assembly Center, and a sample of his senryū composed at the center appears in this anthology. In 1935, the Hokubei Senryū Gosenkai published an anthology of senryū, *Hokubei Senryū*, which was collected and edited by Honda. In 1938, they organized a three-day exhibition in Seattle, which was attended by approximately three thousand people of diverse backgrounds.[44]

As the popularity of senryū grew among the Japanese American Issei, other senryū groups formed in Washington and Oregon, including in Portland, Oregon, where the Bara Ginsha (Rose City) group was organized. Another senryū group in Seattle, Washington, called

Sokoku-kai (Motherland Group) was also active before the war and was led by Jack Yatsutake (pen name Jakki). He was at their senryū meeting when he was arrested by the FBI a few days after the December 7, 1941, Pearl Harbor attack. At the time of his arrest, Yatsutake worked for the Immigration and Naturalization Service as a translator, and the FBI had no evidence to suspect him as a spy. He continued to write senryū while incarcerated in the Justice Department Camp in Crystal City, Texas.[45] His wife and three children were separated from him and imprisoned at the Minidoka camp in Idaho. His daughter is the distinguished poet and academic Mitsuye Yamada, who published his senryū in her collection of poetry, *Camp Notes and Other Poems* (1976). She is still actively writing poetry and promoting multicultural activities.[46]

Haiku groups were also formed at Tule Lake in Northern California. Kenneth Yasuda, a well-known haiku poet and scholar, was incarcerated at Tule Lake. While there, he composed haiku and wrote an article for the March 1943 *Tulean Dispatch Magazine*. His article, "Haiku and Painting" was later incorporated in his well-recognized book, *The Japanese Haiku: Its Essential Nature, History, and Possibilities in English* (1957).

Senryū poets established the Tule Lake Senryū-Kai poetry group shortly after the camp was opened in 1942. This senryū group's activities were well described in a 1945 *Journal of American Folklore* article titled "Senryū Poetry as Folk and Community Expression," by the War Relocation Authority (WRA) community analyst Marvin K. Opler and coauthor Fukuzo Obayashi (a member of the *senryū-kai* group).[47] The group included more than thirty Issei members, including women, and their meetings were held in the "ironing and utility room of block 14, every Tuesday night."[48] Evidence that the crude "*kyōku* mad poem" style of senryū was frowned upon by these modern senryū poets is shown by their rejection (because of its "indecency") of the following senryū:[49]

> oh, incomprehensible!
> in a bachelor's room
> woman's shoes

Despite the members' general feeling of bitterness caused by their incarceration, according to the authors Opler and Obayashi, the senryū poets of Tule Lake did not talk about the war itself at their meetings, but their poems did reflect the social conditions at the camp.[50] Here are three examples from different poets the authors collected:

Women ironing at the Portland Assembly Center. Photo credit: Oregon Historical Society Research Library picture OrHi28163; https://oregonencyclopedia.org/articles/japanese_internment/#.Xt8gZkBFyUk

again, the fingerprints
the old man's
bitter face

on future plans
differences between parent and child
within the fence

the watchtower
where no one can escape
is standing guard

It is important to note that both Opler and Obayashi emphasized the fact that senryū, like haiku, reflect the cultural values of the Issei, who practiced restraint and understatement in their communications. What is left unsaid has the emotional impact on the reader, and the reader must realize that the actual feelings of the poets may be far more intense and bitter. Their urge to satirize is keener, but their expression is culturally restrained.[51]

The United States and Japan were enemies in World War II, but ironically both governments imprisoned senryū and haiku poets. In Japan, when they were at war with China in 1937, a factory worker,

Tsuru Akira (1909–1938), was sent to jail, where he died, for the six senryū he composed protesting the war. One of these senryū is

> no arms or legs—
> they turned the man into a log
> before sending him home[52]

Censorship in Japan increased after the war broke out, and any type of literature criticizing the government's wartime politics was not allowed to be published, including both senryū and haiku.[53] In the late 1930s and throughout World War II, this *kaiko* or *gendai* form of haiku in Japan was seen by pro-nationalist, pro-emperor, and Japanese expansionism supporters as a literary protest movement. Consequently, the modern poets were not approved of by Takahama Kyoshi (also a Shiki student), who, at this time, was the most influential *haijin* (haiku master) in Japan. Kyoshi was the editor of the Japanese haiku journal *Hototogisu*. He was an advocate of structuring haiku with a *kigo* (a season word), *akireji* (a "cut" word indicating a pause), and an element of natural scenery.

During World War II, Kyoshi was the president of the Haiku Branch of the government's culture-control and propaganda group, called The Japanese Literary Patriotic Organization. This group had direct ties to the Imperial government and the Japanese secret police. The Japanese government's disapproval of the new form of haiku came to a head on February 14, 1940, when the Japanese secret police began arresting all the members of Kyôdai Haiku, a Kobe city haiku group. The arrests continued throughout the war, and a total of forty-six haiku poets were imprisoned.[54]

After World War II, the imprisonment of the haiku and senryū poets was considered a war crime by the Japanese government and condemned by many in the Japanese haiku and senryū community.[55] In the United States, the government did not acknowledge the wrongness or racism of the Japanese Americans' incarceration until retribution payments were authorized by President Ronald Reagan in 1989 after the US Congress passed HR 442 in 1988. Additionally, not until 2018 did Supreme Court Justice John Roberts state, "The forcible relocation of U.S. citizens to concentration camps based solely on race is objectively unlawful."[56]

When the war ended and the incarcerated Japanese American senryū poets returned home, they continued to gather and hold club meetings. The poets published their senryū in Japanese American newspapers and in Japanese-language senryū journals. One of the journals was the *Senryū Bara*, which was published in Portland, Oregon, under the leadership of its editor, Mrs. Hisako Saito (pen name Ryūko), who was also a member of the Bara Ginsha Senryū group in Portland.

In 1972, an intercultural exchange senryū conference was held in Portland, Oregon, and included a group of senryū poets from Japan. One of the topics discussed was the need to translate into English the senryū written by Japanese American poets. This was partly due to the realization that the senryū translations by R. H. Blyth that appear in *Japanese Life and Character in Senryū* (1960) did not reflect well enough the *gendai senryū* (modern senryū) philosophy and the Japanese poets who rejected the "dirty joke" *ko-senryū* of the Kyōku period (1824–1900).[57]

Mr. Kōyō Satō, a member of the Hokubei Senryū group in Olympia, Washington, began organizing an effort to have modern senryū translated for the English-speaking public. Satō, with the help of Shigenobu Nagai, the Japanese consulate general of Japan in Seattle, and together with the local Japanese American Citizens' League, recruited Dr. John Michio Ohno (pen name Shūhō) to provide the translations. This collection of senryū was first introduced at the 1981 Evergreen State College Japanese cultural festival.

In 1987, Dr. John Michio Ohno, using his pen name of Shūhō Ohno, published the book *Modern Senryu in English*. The first part of the book includes a history of senryū, outlines its characteristics, and introduces 433 translations of modern senryū by Japanese Americans in the United States. Poets in the Ohno anthology who are also represented in this anthology are Masaki Kinoshita (Jōnan), Shinjiro Honda (Kahō), Kurokawa (Kentsuku), Kyokuo Ito (Uson), Shigeru Mihara (Gochi), and Toyoko Tamura (Shinsetsu). The second part of the Ohno book is a guide to writing senryū in English for English speakers.[58]

Currently, some active Japanese American senryū and haiku groups in the United States still write their poetry in Japanese. The Japanese American community continues to keep alive the memories of the injustices suffered by their families incarcerated during World War II.[59] In recent times, many Japanese Americans have protested the treatment of Central and South American immigrants to the United States, as they and others see behind those cages and barbed wire the same injustices their own families have experienced. Readers of the senryū in this anthology should try to keep in their mind's eye the locations and conditions under which the senryū were written. Remember the flies.

Shelley Baker-Gard
Portland, Oregon, 2021

About the Translations

When we started working on these poems, we found their poignancy to be startling, even shocking. The manifold uncertainties that the incarcerated Japanese Americans endured were palpable, even in the first poem we looked at (no. 65 in this volume):

> melancholy laughter
> helps us pass the time
> until the train departs

Translating these poems was an education in empathy every bit as much as it was an exercise in the Japanese language.

These poems were written in 1942, and the ages of the poets varied widely. Kurokawa was eighty, Kinoshita was forty-six, and Saito, a relative youngster, was only twenty-nine. Some of the writers of these poems were experienced at writing senryū. Many were not. However, they were all ordinary people, trying to make the best of the unbearable. Their feelings are often expressed directly, and with a raw intensity.

Translation is more of an art than a science. Any translation involves threading the needle between literal fidelity to the original text and comprehensibility to people coming from another culture. Even at the most elementary level—say, the meaning of an individual word—these challenges arise. Few words in any language are so simple that their "dictionary definition" suffices to capture their entire meaning, let alone the nuances embedded in what we might call the word's "street definition."

With the Japanese language in particular, additional challenges are presented by the variations in orthography that are mixed together. These include the pictographic characters (kanji) derived from Chinese, the syllabic script (hiragana) used primarily for expressions and syntactic features native to original Japanese, and an additional syllabic script (katakana) used primarily for foreign words, intense expressions, and various forms of onomatopoeia. Each of these scripts has unique features that need to be taken into account.

With literary translations, an additional source of tension is thrown into the mix—the need to use forms and conventions of recognizable literary quality in the target language. In navigating the tension between literal clarity and literary style, translators often find themselves gravitating toward a particular approach, and even good translators may find themselves occupying very different points along this multidimensional spectrum.

In all, we can group the challenges into four basic categories: the historical context, the Japanese language, Japanese poetic style, and the use of kanji and kana. We discuss each in detail below.

The Historical Context

In any historical period, a community will be conscious of the context that shapes their current condition. It may include incidents that occur locally and are referred to without a specific name, because everybody knows what is being talked about. It may also include known historical events that have little lasting importance. Many of them, if not most, will fade from memory as time goes on.

An example of the former is the event referred to in the phrase "since it happened" in poem no. 59 (in the section titled "Doubt" in this volume). The lack of a specific referent for this event could be attributed to several possible factors. Perhaps the poet felt there was insufficient space in the seventeen syllables (known as *on* in Japanese) of a senryū to delineate it adequately. Or the event might have been so shocking and traumatic that a more direct reference would violate the poet's customary reticence to refer to things too directly.

In the absence of a clear and unambiguous referent, the translator is forced to guess. Perhaps it was some altercation between teenagers at the center. Possibly it was an action by one or more of the guards, such as the obviously traumatic event of August 15, 1942, just a week or two before the poem was written. As related by George Katagiri, "One day, a Military Police cook came through the gate to borrow food items from the center's kitchen. A Military Police guard shot him in broad daylight—a sobering sight for the internees." [1] Our ignorance of the exact nature of the incident referred to in the poem prevents us from expressing its emotional impact with complete precision. Consequently, we must content ourselves with the relatively bland, but close to literal, expression "I watch more closely."

An example of a recent event of historical significance to the Japanese immigrants, yet now mostly forgotten by all but Japanese history scholars, is the reference to Hill 203 in poem 39 (in the section titled "About Anything," August 22). The referent in this case is a hill in Dalian, China, dubbed "203" because it was 203 meters high. During the siege of Port Arthur in the Russo-Japanese war, it was the site of several bloody battles between Russian and Japanese troops in September and October of 1904, in which the Japanese lost thousands of men.

As with bloody battles from other wars, such as Gettysburg, Pork Chop Hill, or Balaclava in Crimea (which spawned "The Charge of the Light Brigade"), Hill 203 became the stuff of heroic legend, while at the same time serving as an object lesson in the horrors and depredations of war. The Japanese commander, General Nogi, for example, was moved to pen this eulogy, mixing a classical Chinese style with a direct quotation from Otto von Bismarck's 1862 remark that "blood and iron" were the decisive elements in geopolitical struggle.

> Hard it was to climb this hill
> Men were seeking honor, men made it so
> Transformed by blood and iron
> All gaze upward now at this mountain
> Where souls fell like rain

Although this event occurred almost forty years prior to the writing of poem no. 39, it must have been still in the minds of some of the detainees at the North Portland Assembly Center, perhaps as a result of history lessons from their Japanese school days. Some Issei at the assembly center may even have had relatives who perished in the battle.

Oddly, this senryū uses the battlefield of Hill 203 to describe a mother's hairstyle. The humorous irony was probably intended to elicit a laugh. Hopefully it was taken in that spirit. But this does not reduce the challenge for the translator when an event may not be known to the contemporary reader. Generic references, such as "a battlefield" lack the requisite emotional punch. So, we opted simply for a direct reference to Hill 203, relying on an explanatory footnote to provide further information.

Finally, in considering the historical context, we must talk about the conditions under which this manuscript was produced. Material written in Japanese, and therefore inaccessible to the guards, was generally forbidden. Masaki Kinoshita was perhaps taking a risk in compiling this journal of the senryū-kai. If so, recording the poems may have been a hurried, or even furtive, affair, increasing the likelihood of transcription errors and omissions.

The Japanese Language

One of the salient features of Japanese grammar, compared to English, is its comparative flexibility in labeling the participants in an action or event. A properly constructed English sentence requires a subject (imperatives excepted) and an object (if the verb is transitive), and requires other participants to be embedded appropriately in prepositional phrases or subordinate clauses.

The labeling system is quite different in Japanese. Many more participants in an expression can be, and often are, omitted. This occurs more frequently in poetry than in prose of course, in part due to the seventeen-syllable (*on*) limit, which encourages brevity. But it also dovetails neatly with a traditional Japanese preference for indirect communication that leans heavily on context for meaning. What is not said is often as important as what is said. The absence of elements of an expression or thought that are required for an English translation, of course, poses an additional set of challenges for the translator.

To begin with, the subject of a Japanese sentence does not need to be stated. Most often it is not stated at all. When it is stated, it usually appears as the topic, or focus of attention, and is labeled by the *hiragana ha* ((は)), which is pronounced as *wa* when employed to signal the topic of a sentence. The formal label for the subject of a verb, *ga* (が), typically appears only in embedded clauses. In some cases, for example no. 29, the subject is relatively clear from context. In others, such as no. 20, it is unclear whether the poet is referring to themselves, or to someone else, or, as in no. 33, whether the implied subject is singular or plural in addition to the first person / third person ambiguity. Less frequently, even the main verb is not stated. Poem no. 25 provides an example, in which the final clause *tsuma e dake* ("only to my wife") omits the verb. In cases like this, a suitable verb (here, "whispered") needs to be added.

In a similar vein, while Japanese has clear first-person pronouns for I (*watashi*, *boku*, and so on) and third-person pronouns for "him" (*kare*) and "her" (*kanojo*), as well as their possessive variants, such qualified references are often omitted in Japanese, leaving it unclear even whether the referent is first person or third person, male or female. In a few cases where we can make a plausible guess, we opted for a choice that would make the poem suitably concrete. In most cases, however, we have confined ourselves to more generic terms like "such" (no. 8) or "child" (no. 33), even though their emotional impact is somewhat attenuated.

Sometimes, these ambiguities compound themselves to the point where a senryū may support multiple different interpretations. Poem no. 18 is an example, where the inability to accept his father's "blind spot" or "hot button" could be attributed either to the father himself, or to the poet, Masaki Kinoshita.

Poem no. 1 presents us with another example. The first line of the poem refers to "giving up" or abandoning some effort, followed by *keredo* ("however"), which implies that what follows (an "unbreakable" or karmic connection) is a contrary notion. This presents us with a puzzle to decipher. Is the poet abandoning the effort to establish or maintain a connection, only to discover that it cannot be broken, or is *keredo* intended as a dismissal of his own puny efforts in the face of something much larger?

Yet another example occurs in poem no. 3. To set the scene, two Japanese immigrants at the detention center discover that they have the same hometown. One asks the other "your neighborhood?" The poet characterizes this interaction as *natsukashisa*, a word similar to our own "nostalgia," but with much more powerful connotations of affection and longing. Translators have differed as to whether this nostalgia applies to the question itself, or to the (unspoken) answer. We resolved this conflict in favor of the answer. The name of a neighborhood where one spent time in one's youth, say "Southie," or "Washington Heights," or "Visitacion Valley," seems to invoke a much more powerful emotional response than the question on its own.

Poem no. 29 provides an example where in the ambiguity also carries over into English. Neither the subject nor the object is identified explicitly. The omitted subject is almost certainly "I," in standard Japanese usage, but the omitted object could be either the second person singular ("you dearest") or plural ("you all"). In the first case, this poem can be read as a touching declaration of love—the Japanese have always viewed dying together in the most romantic terms. In the second case, it can be read as an ironic, even sarcastic, rejoinder to no. 23: "And I've come all this way, just to die with you." Between 1907 and 1920, Japanese women immigrants came to the United States only as "picture brides," arranged for via correspondence and through relatives in Japan, and it's possible that the poet has chosen to adopt the voice of one of these picture brides in attempting to articulate the futility of life in the camp.

Interestingly, another feature of the Japanese language occasionally helps us to disambiguate the poem. One convention of Japanese politeness is to use different expressions when talking about oneself or one's family than when talking about others. The latter type of expression is inevitably more respectful, while the former is more humble, a syntactic form of linguistic self-denigration.

For example, one would refer to another's wife, or any married woman as *okusan* (奥さん), while referring to one's own as *tsuma* (妻). Uses of the *tsuma* are found in poems no. 9, no. 13, no. 15, and no. 25 by Masaki Kinoshita. Kinoshita appears to have written several of his poems in the "voice" of another detainee, so these poems may or may not refer to his own spouse. But we can be pretty sure they are intended to refer to the spouse of the persona in whose voice the poem is written. Even in senryū no. 24, which appears to take the form of an aphorism, it is at least a reasonable guess that the aphorism is intended to character-ize Shousui's own wife.

The Japanese language also presents challenges that are not neces-sarily unique to Japanese, but common to any translation effort. Most basic, perhaps, is the question of the meaning of an individual word. The student of any language, including Japanese, quickly discovers that nearly every word encompasses a variety of meanings and nuances that are not adequately explained, or even accounted for, in the word's "dictionary definition." In particular, what we might call a word's "street definition" can often change the dictionary definition by adding certain nuances, or even changing the usage of a word entirely, in a way that can even vary from epoch to epoch. English is no exception. Consider, for example, the use of the words "wicked" and "bad" in a colloquial expression like "He blows that sax with a wicked bad energy," in which the words are used in a fashion that is nearly the opposite of their dictionary definition.

We encounter these issues in several poems. In poem no. 5, for example, the first word, *kaki,* has a dictionary definition of "fence." The context of this poem, however, provides additional information about the nature of this fence. The assembly center was in essence a prison, so we've chosen the term "barbed wire" to accentuate this point, adding to the pathos of the poem for an English reader. Also in this same poem, the word *shimiru* is associated with dictionary definitions like "pierce," "pen-etrate," "permeate," but when applied to one's eyes, it implies a certain amount of pain, which could range from something as mild as "smart-ing" to "burning" and even "stabbing." A conventional interpretation, which would imply tears or the act of crying, might be literally correct in the sense that it is the tears that are penetrating and permeating the eyes. But such a translation would not adequately bring out this painful aspect. Consequently, we have opted for the stronger word of "stinging."

In poem no. 9, the term *arau* literally means to wash. What is being washed in the context of this poem, however, is emotional rather than physical. His wife is disguising her true emotions, which the poet doesn't disclose, behind a mask of nonchalance. The English word "wash" simply won't work in this context, so we've opted for "baffling."

Poem no. 12 exhibits a different type of ambiguity, related to the implied scope of the main verb. The poet refers to the fact that he can no longer observe (*mirarenu*) his father's habits since coming to the Portland Assembly Center. It is not clear from the text of the poem, however, whether this is because the poet's father has changed his habits, or because the poet's father is not in the same location. In this case, we relied on contextual information from poem no. 4, where the same poet (Jōnan) nostalgically refers to his father's "happy drunken song" as further evidence that the poet and his father have been separated by the vicissitudes of incarceration.

In some cases, it is necessary to look into the etymology of a word in order to divine its intended meaning within a specific poem. Take poem no. 66, for instance. The poet is expressing his gratitude at being forgiven for being *wagamama*. Dictionary definitions of the word tend to cover a wide spectrum—selfish, egotistical, willful, self-indulgent, and so on.

With such a broad spectrum of possible meanings, it becomes difficult to pin down exactly what sort of selfishness or self-indulgence is being forgiven. But if we deconstruct the term into its constituent parts of *waga* ("my," "mine"), and *mama* ("as is," "as one likes"), we see that a particular type of selfishness is implied by this combination—namely wanting things done in one's own way. This leads to a simpler and more directly meaningful interpretation: the poet is being forgiven for insisting too aggressively on doing things in his own particular way.

Japanese Poetic Style

Senryū-kai and *haiku-kai* are social gatherings during which the members each contribute their own poems. The poems are sometimes composed independently, sometimes in a sequence. Quite often, contests are held in which winning haiku or senryū are selected by a panel of judges, or by an individual master poet who is frequently the leader of the group, or by a vote of the attendees (see "Introduction" and "American English Senryū and Haiku" for more information).

Many gatherings at the assembly center were organized by the Japanese Americans themselves, to maintain morale by holding social events that would provide enjoyment, shared experience, and a distraction from the fears and anxieties of life in the center. The *senryū-kai* meetings were no exception, but they served additional purposes as well, providing a means for cultural enrichment and allowing the poets an outlet for expressing their emotions and frustrations. Like literary activity of any sort, they afforded participants the space to gain some detachment from their feelings even while processing them in a conscious, "non-triggering" (or at least "less triggering") mode.

The social context of *senryū-kai* also opens up the possibility that the poets occasionally employed modalities of expression that depended on this social context. Expressions that imply meaning beyond the words are found in many of the senryū. These include irony (no. 21, no. 38, no. 47), exaggeration for effect (no. 8, no. 29), outright sarcasm (no. 32), or even possible jokes (no. 4, no. 13, no. 39).

Another adaptation to social exigencies is the use of literary or quasi-literary symbolism in creating more "artistic" portrayals of emotion (no. 5, no. 6), enabling the poet to express their emotions at a certain level of aesthetic distance, thus making them more acceptable in a social situation. In poem no. 6, for example, Saito uses the phrase *to iu kanji* ("such a feeling") to create a space between herself and the almost paradoxical emotion of beginning to feel at home in such an otherwise uncongenial place.

Japanese poetry permits grammatical constructs that provide additional flexibility in meeting the seventeen-syllable (*on*) constraint. Expressive particles like *ya* (や) do not add to the content of the description so much as indicate the poet's emotional response by way of emphasis. Often, they are used as *kireji* ("cutting words") to separate the poem into two parts. Recall Bashō's famous line, *furu ike ya* ("This old pond!"), where *ya* plays a role similar to the way we might employ an exclamation point in English. Other syllables that express emotional nuances include *ka* (か), *sa* (さ), and *na* (な). An example can be found in senryū no. 27. Expressive particles are also commonly heard in everyday speech.

Another construct, less commonly found in ordinary speech, is the use of the single syllables, such as *nu* (ぬ) or *zu* (ず) to negate a verb, which conserves one syllable when compared to the much more common spoken alternatives such as *nai* (ない) or *naku* (なく). Examples of this construction can be seen in no. 7, no. 9, no. 10, no. 17, no. 18, no. 33, no. 40, no. 51, no. 53, no. 55, no. 57, no. 58, no. 61, no. 64, and no. 67.

Finally, haiku and senryū often use verb forms that do not correspond directly to an English verb tense. Most commonly, these verb forms end with an "I" sound, such as *iki* (no. 45), *ari* (no. 48), and *nigiri* (no. 51, no. 52). In some cases, this verb form corresponds to the English "ing" form, indicating a present participle. In others, it indicates completion of one action in a sequence. Or it can simply be a poetic stand-in for a fully tensed verb, possibly saving a syllable or two, at the cost of ambiguity as to whether the action is now occurring or has already occurred.

Additional examples of this verb form are found throughout the manuscript, including senryū no. 19, no. 22, no. 26, no. 27, no. 30, no. 32, no. 36, no. 42, no. 43, no. 44, and no. 56. In fact, this usage occurs so commonly that fully tensed verbs (e.g., no. 29) appear to be the rarities. In each case, we must make a judgment from context regarding the most appropriate verb tense for translation, since a verb without a tense marker does not usually make sense in English. Even present participles typically indicate ongoing, if incomplete, activity.

Like poets writing in any language, Japanese poets are fond of allusions to well-known writings that came before. We don't find a huge number of allusions in the assembly center poems, but we do find a few, such as in poem no. 30, whose sentiments should be well known to anyone who completed elementary school in Japan, including many of our poets.

Japanese schoolchildren are typically expected to memorize the opening lines of the "Heike Monogatari," a chronicle of the battles between the Taira and Minamoto clans that signaled the end of the Heian period and the transfer of effective power from the imperial court to a succession of military governors, or shoguns, that would continue until 1868. The opening passage of this "Tale of the Heike" is translated by Helen Craig McCullough as follows: "The sound of the Gion Shōja bells echoes the impermanence of all things; the color of the *sāla* flowers reveal the truth that the prosperous must decline. The proud do not endure, they are like a dream on a spring night; the mighty fall at last, they are as dust before the wind."[2] The sentiment in senryu no. 30 likewise evokes the idea that what was once great is destined to fall.

The Use of Kanji and Kana

The Japanese written language combines three different sets of symbols: hiragana, katakana, and kanji. Hiragana and katakana both identify single syllables of the spoken language, with a one-to-one correspondence between them. In other words, every hiragana character has a corresponding katakana character, and vice versa. Hiragana are used almost exclusively for native Japanese words, while katakana are used primarily to indicate the pronunciation of foreign loan words. Kanji are ideographic characters, originally imported from China, although the orthography of many kanji have diverged from the Chinese over the years, as both countries followed independent paths in an effort to simplify them.

Not until after the war, in 1946, did the Japanese government establish the "official" Toyo Kanji, in an attempt to standardize and simplify the characters used in everyday written Japanese. Consequently, the written kanji in these poems differs in some cases from modern Japanese usage. Examples can be found in senryū no. 3, no. 4, no. 7, and no. 10.

In some cases, the conventional form of the kanji is abbreviated for convenience in writing. An example occurs in poem no. 67, where the handwritten manuscript appears to indicate the kanji 向 (*mukou*, or "over there"), but the actual intent is to abbreviate the character 問 (*tou*, or "ask about"). The same shorthand is employed in a different character—the final character for *matsuma* (間) in poem no. 40, which indicates a period of time.

These differences in orthography also extend beyond the kanji themselves, to include issues related to the use of kana. Many of the poems employ archaic conventions for both short and elongated vowel sounds, by using the "h" (or "f" in the case of "fu") hiragana, rather than the hiragana for the isolated vowel. Examples include "fu" (ふ) instead of "u" (う) (no. 14), "he" (へ) instead of "e" (え) (no. 32, no. 49, no. 60), and "hi" (ひ) instead of "i" (い) (no. 52, no. 57, no. 63, no. 65, no. 67).

Katakana, typically used to record foreign (mainly English) words, can also pose challenges. In some cases, the intended foreign word is clear. For instance, in poem no. 5, the word ネオン can be easily identified as "neon," and, in no. 41, ホット indicates "hot."

Other foreign words were more difficult to identify and required a certain amount of research into source materials describing the center. For example, in poem no. 45, we were able to determine that ビーツ ("beets") refers to certain beet fields in Idaho, where many individuals and families volunteered their labor to escape the assembly center; many remained in Idaho after the war.

Poem no. 48 presents another interesting case, where チト ("chito") appears to be a shortened version of "notchit," a word invented by the Japanese Americans. The word describes the wood chips that are produced when sticks are notched to indicate the passage of time during incarceration. Whether that makes the word English or Japanese is an interesting question, but either way, the use of katakana makes perfect sense.

To compound the complexity of identifying foreign words, katakana are also used on occasion to spell out Japanese words, using the katakana to provide a sense of emphasis. In poem no. 49, for example, the word ホロリ (*horori*) is a Japanese word that means being moved to tears.

Poetry aims at the evocative rather than the merely literal or logical. Moods and feelings are its medium, and poets frequently use metaphors and allusions (phrases intended to recall other poems or stories) to accomplish this, by calling in thoughts and recollections from outside the poem itself to enhance its emotional richness. Phrases such as "slings and arrows" or "out, damned spot" readily evoke the emotional complexities of Hamlet and Macbeth, respectively.

In Japanese, a single Chinese character can conjure up not just one but many different allusions, depending on how it has been used in the past. The example of *miyako* in poem no. 6 is illustrative. Attempting to express her increasing acclimatization to the surroundings of the center, Ryūko (Hisako Saito) invokes the Japanese idiom *sumeba miyako*—literally, "if you live there, it is the capital"—to express the contentment and satisfaction found in one's own dwelling place. Though born in Oregon, Ryūko actually spent much of her childhood in Japan before returning to the United States. This helps explain her facility with Japanese idioms.

But the kanji for *miyako* may bring with it any of a host of recollections from Japanese history. The happy hustle and bustle of the modern-day capital of Tokyo, to be sure, but more richly, this character will also recall the ancient city of Kyoto— the deep spirituality of its many temples and shrines, dazzling memories of the Heian court, and the legends of bravery and heroism in the rivalry between the Taira and the Minamoto clans. In short, a deep nostalgia for the grace and glamour of that classical period, when the word *miyako* was essentially synonymous with Kyoto. It is not unreasonable to think of Kyoto as the spiritual "home" of the Japanese people, which helps to compound the depth of Saito's expression.

Calligraphy of the Japanese idiom sumeba miyako— literally, "if you live there, it is the capital." Permission to use the photograph was granted by the owner, Ken Klein.

The illustration on the right shows a Japanese calligraphy scroll of the *sumeba miyako* idiom.

An interesting contrast in the use of kanji versus katakana is found in the way the assembly center itself is referred to. In senryū no. 47, Masaki Kinoshita (Jōnan) uses katakana (センター or "*senta*"—), which is largely free from associations native to Japan, and carries with it a distinctly Western connotation.

Using the kanji sequence (*shuugousho*) to refer to the assembly center creates a different effect, as shown in senryū no. 6 by Ryūko (Hisako Saito) and in senryū no. 12 and no. 46 by Jōnan (Masaki Kinoshita): 収合所 could evoke memories of the historical bureaucracies of feudal Japan and establish a common link between bureaucratic processes in both countries, as if to emphasize the similarities between their current environment and their former Japanese home. This is particularly apt in Saito's poem, given the additional link to her home in *sumeba miyako*, as discussed above.

In Conclusion

As Dr. John Michio Ohno advises, "Translation of senryū is difficult if there are many different ways of interpreting each poem. The translator must consider the background, age, gender, education, and experience of the author of each poem. Most importantly, the understanding of the poet's intention is critical." As editors of this collection, we have spent many hours researching the contextual information and experiences of the poets represented. We have worked to provide the most accurate interpretation we could come up with for each poem.

Nevertheless, as Ohno also states, "There is no one 'correct' translation if there are too many implications in the original *senryū*."[3] Given the incompleteness of historical or personal information, and the fact that over eighty years have elapsed since 1942, there are bound to be some misunderstandings, and alternative interpretations that are preferred by some readers. We apologize in advance for these.

In summary, coming up with adequate translations of these poems requires a sensitivity to the cultural differences between literary efforts in English and Japanese, combined with research into some of the more obscure references and events that these poets frequently refer to. Trade-offs must frequently be made, and one can only hope that the results do justice to both the intent and the feelings of the original poets.

Mike Freiling

SENRYŪ

ポートランド川柳句集吟社

HOLLAND LINEN
FINISH

Connections

August 8, 1942

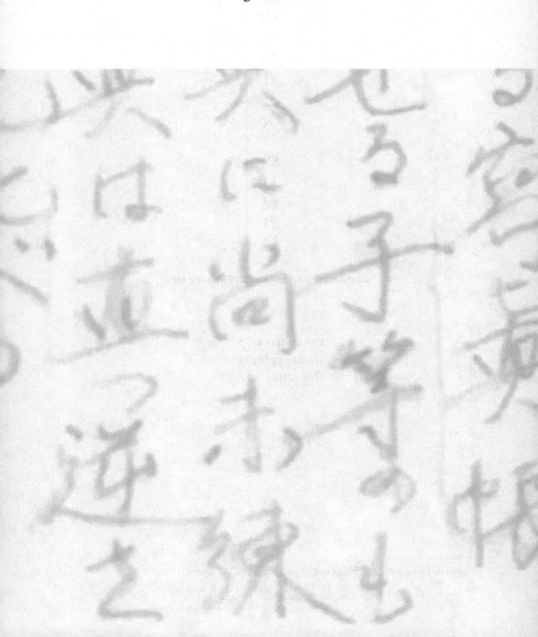

1

by Jōnan

諦めて居れど矢っ張り腐れ縁

akiramete oredo yappari kusare en

my efforts stop
no use fighting
this rotten fate[*]

---

[*] Literal: I give it up, *kusare* is a rotten-bad scent (p. 2 of journal).

2

by Jōnan

無
い
縁
と
泣
い
て
わ
か
れ
た
一
昔

naien to naite wakareta hito mukashi

destined never to connect
I mourn our parting
so long ago*

---

*Literal: Though we parted ages ago, I still cry over our lack of connection (p. 2 of journal).

3

by Hisataro

故郷のどの辺と聞く懐かしさ

furusato no dono hen to kiku natsukashi sa

your neighborhood?
from the same hometown—
memories*

---

*Literal: Where in our hometown are you from? We ask nostalgically (p. 3 of journal).
The character for *hen* has been simplified since these were written.

Talking About Anything

August 8, 1942

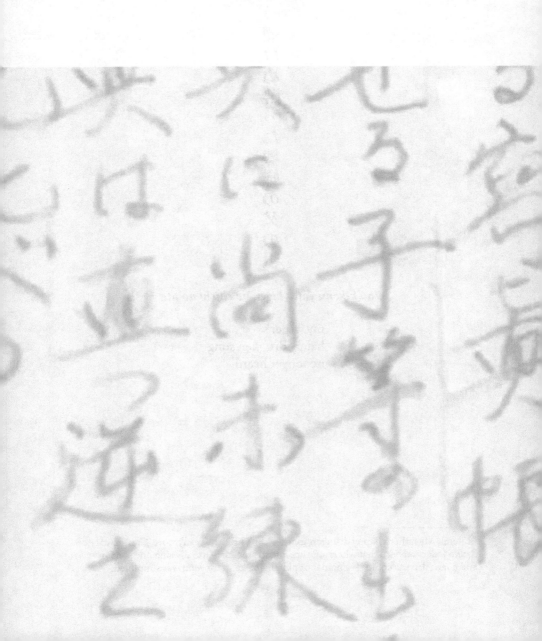

4

by Jōnan

もう聞けぬ酔った機嫌の父の唄

mou kikenu yotta kigen no chichi no uta

my father's
happy drunken song
no longer heard*

---

* Literal: My father's happy drunken songs—can't hear them anymore. Contextual note: Rinko Jeffers advised that when men are intoxicated, they usually sing one song over and over. Also *uta* could be singular or plural. The kanji for *yotta* was simplified.

5

by Jōnan

垣のそと燃ゆるネオンが瞳にしみる

kaki no soto moyuru "neon" ga me ni shimiru

beyond the barbed wire
a glow of neon lights
stinging my eyes*

---

* Literal: Outside the fence, glow of neon signs—tears in my eyes (p. 4 of journal). "Tears in my eyes" in Japanese implies a question as to why tears are welling up. The character for "eye" specifically refers to the pupil of the eye and is read *hitomi* or *dou*, but we elected to pronounce it as *me* (eye), because it fits the 5-7-5 pattern better, and also because *me nishimiru* is a common Japanese expression.

6

by Ryūko

収
合
所
住
め
ば
都
と
云
ふ
感
じ

shuugousho sumeba miyako to iu kanji

starting to feel
perfectly at home
here in the Center*

---

* Literal: The assembly center has the feeling we call "where you live is the capital."
Translation note: The expression *sumebamiyako* literally means "where you live is the capital." It is a Japanese idiom for expressing delight in your current residence. For more discussion of this phrase, see the "Use of Kanji and Kana" section in "About the Translations."

7

by Jōnan

姑
の
腑
に
落
ち
ぬ
は
嫁
の
育
児
法

shuutome no fu ni ochinu wa yome no iku ji ho

with eyebrows up
mother-in-law watches
how she raises them*

---

*Literal: Incomprehensible to grandmother—her way of raising children (p. 4 of the journal). The character for *ji* has been simplified.

Sensibility and Discretion

August 8, 1942

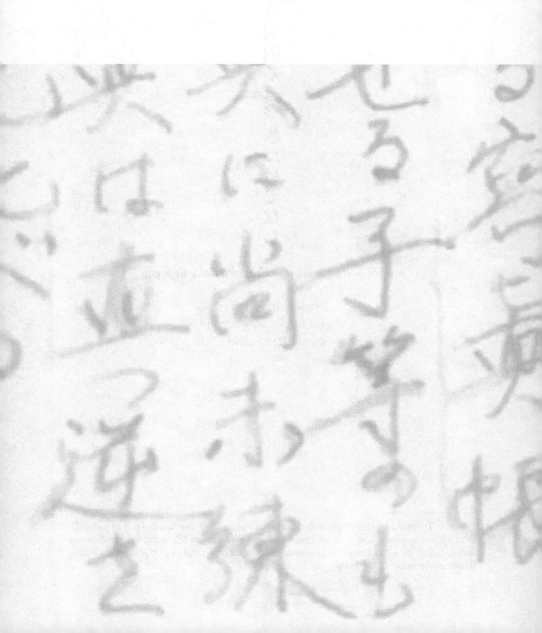

8

by Jōnan

無分別困るは家族だけでなし

mufun betsu komaru wa kazoku dake de nashi

trouble maker
for family and beyond—
such indiscretion*

---

* Literal: Troubled by lack of consideration—not just within the family (p. 5 of journal).
Rinko Jeffers suggests this is about a person, *betsu*, who doesn't know the right and wrong
way to act as far as traditional ways, both inside the family and in public, and is causing
shame and trouble to the family and community.

9

by Jōnan

分
別
は
あ
ら
う
と
妻
は
知
ら
ぬ
顔

fun betsu wa arou to tsuma wa shiranu kao

not a trouble maker
despite my wife's face—
so baffling*

---

*Literal: I know my wife is considerate—despite her inscrutable face (p. 5 of journal). In 1942, the word *arou* was written *arau* but pronounced *arou*.

10

by Jōnan

簡単に往かぬと母は義理を説く

kantan ni ikanu to haha wa giri wo toku

my mother says
"things are not so simple"
duty beckons*

---

*Literal: When my mother says, "things are not so simple," she's talking about one's duty (obligations). Second character of *kantan* has been simplified since this poem was written.

11

by Jōnan

簡
単
に
出
来
な
い
話
人
を
立
て

kantan ni dekinai hanashi hito wo tate

to an elder
you talk around it first—
that is respect*

---

*Literal: cannot speak simply—respect the person. Alternative translation: one never speaks too directly if one truly respects one's superiors.

Habits

August 15, 1942

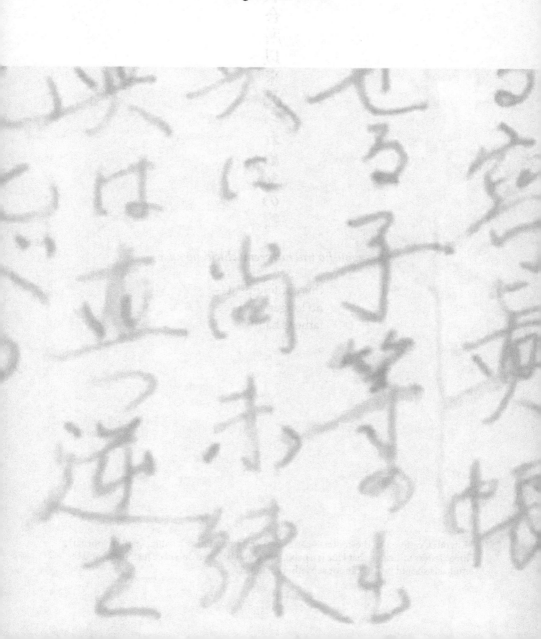

12

by Jōnan

収
合
所
以
来
見
ら
れ
ぬ
父
の
癖

shuugousho irai mirarenu chichi no kuse

this confinement—
no longer can I see
father's habits*

---

* Literal: Confined to the center—can't keep an eye on father's habits (p. 8 of journal).
Rinko Jeffers indicated that *kuse* is a habit that could be good or bad or just funny, and the
emphasis should be on "cannot see father's habits."

13

by Jōnan

妻の留守それから甘え癖をつけ

tsuma no rusu sorekara amaeguse wo tsuke

my wife's absence—
lapsing into habits
of self-indulgence*

---

*Literal: Wife is gone—sinking into "spoiled child" habits. The term *amae* refers to the spoiled dependence often exhibited by young children in relation to their parents (p. 9 of journal).

14

by Jōnan

指
を
吸
ふ
癖
も
な
つ
か
し
幼
い
日

yubi wo suu kuse mo natsukashi osanai hi

toddler's habit
security from a thumb—
easy for them*

---

* Literal: Nostalgia for a small child's habits—like sucking one's thumb (craving that feeling of safety of a small child) (p. 9 of journal).

15

by Jōnan

妻の癖子が出来てから目立って来

tsuma no kuse ko ga dekite kara medatte ki

my wife's habits
after our baby's birth
are more apparent*

---

*Literal: Wife's habit—since she had a baby—has become obvious (now I can under-
stand my wife's habit of relaxing with the baby). The meaning of *ki* at the end would
normally be pronounced *kita* (past tense of *kuru*) but the *ta* was dropped to fit the 5-7-5
senryū pattern.

16

by Jōnan

三ヶ月二人の癖が出る時分

san ka getsu futari no kuse ga deru jibun

after three months
newlyweds begin to have
their habits*

---

*Literal: Three months—habits of a couple—starting to come out (the habits they had just three months after becoming a couple are starting to appear). Translation note: The final "n" hiragana was omitted in the manuscript. Contextual note: The *Evacuazette* reported in its June 23 edition that Mr. and Mrs. Milton Maeda celebrated their one-month wedding anniversary with a small party.

17

by Roshyou

扉
な
し
の
生
活
続
け
て
愚
痴
も
出
ず

tobira nashi no seikatsu tsuzukete guchi mo dezu

life continues
in rooms without doors
complaints unheard*

---

* Literal: Even as our way of life without doors (without privacy) continues, complaints are not heard. Translation note: The term *guchi* has Buddhist overtones of *moha* or *maya*—folly, ignorance, mistaking daily frustrations for the ultimate reality. The term *dezu* is a negative form of *deru*, indicating a failure to emerge, or come about. Contextual note: The *Evacuazette* reported on the need for people to be quiet after 10 p.m. to allow for sleep. People did complain about the lack of privacy and there were cartoons depicting this. It is likely the complaints did not particularly concern the WCCA Administration (i.e., complaints mattered so little, they did not exist).

About Anything

August 15, 1942

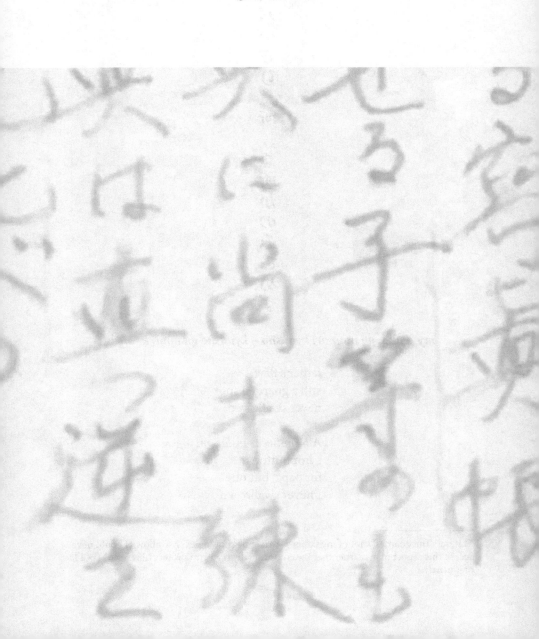

18

by Jōnan

パパの守り急所、急所がのみこめず

my 'Papa' no mamori kyuusho – kyuusho ga nomi komezu

father's flaw
still a guarded spot—
never swallowed

Alternative translation:
a hot button
for papa, but one
I never swallowed*

---

* Literal: The guarded spot of my father—that spot I could never swallow (I could never accept this aspect of my father that I was continually trying to protect him from) (p. 11 of journal).

19

by Jōnan

壁越しに挨拶してる國訛り

kabe goshi ni aisatsu shiteru kuni namari

across the wall
we exchange greetings
in our own dialects*

---

*Literal: Separated by the wall—we greet each other—in our native dialect (p. 11 of journal).

20

by Jōnan

子
を
呼
べ
ば
此
の
日
盛
り
を
砂
の
上

ko wo yobeba kono hi zakari wo suna no ue

I called my kid
playing today at noon
just dirt clouds her*

---

*Literal: Calling my kid—today at noon—playing in the dirt. (Possibly a meditation on
the untroubled life of a child, even amid such chaos) (p. 11 of journal).

21

by Jōnan

よ
う
よ
う
と
歩
け
て
母
の
忙
し
さ

you you to arukete haha no isogashisa

cheery mother
here there and all about
not thinking on where*

---

*Literal: Light of step—mother can pop around (she is bustling about her business apparently untroubled and joyful) (p. 11 of journal).

22

by Souu

住
み
馴
れ
た
頃
へ
移
動
の
噂
立
ち

sumi nareta koro e idou no uwasa tachi

just settled in—
now rumors cropping up
of the move ahead*

---

*Literal: Just when we've become accustomed to living here, they talk about moving us.
Translation note: The term *uwasa tachi* literally means "the rumor stands up," an idiom
for starting or beginning. Contextual note: At the end of July 1942, the *Evacuazette*
reported on the rumors in the assembly center concerning the move. Not until August
19 did they receive the official notification on which families were to be incarcerated
at the Minidoka camp in Idaho and which were going to the Heart Mountain camp in
Wyoming.

Resolution and Readiness

August 16, 1942

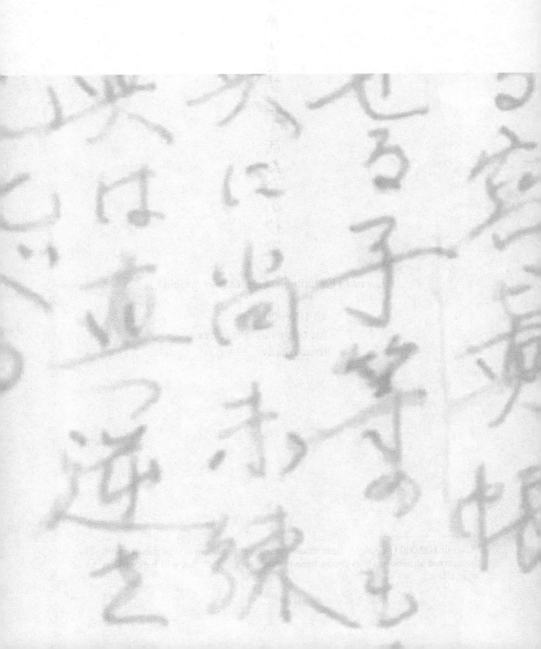

23

by Jōnan

十
萬
が
覚
悟
し
て
居
た
今
の
位
置

juu man ga kakugo shite ita ima no ichi

all 100,000 of us
for these current times
made ready*

---

*Literal: 100,000 (people)—have made themselves ready (to accept their condition)—the current situation. (Everybody here is ready to accept what will happen) (p. 13 of journal).

24

by Shousui

やわらかい妻に覚悟が又とかれ

yawarakai tsuma ni kakugo ga mata tokare

nonchalant wife
has not yet arrived
at resolution*

---

*Literal: To an easy-going wife, resolution is not yet accomplished.

25

by Jōnan

萬一の覚悟をしろと妻へだけ

man ichi no kakugo wo shiro to tsuma e dake

if the worst happens
resolve to persevere—
whispered to my wife*

---

*Literal: Most unlikely possibility—persevere resolution—only to my wife (Only to my wife I say "Persevere in your resolution even if the worst should happen") (p. 13 of journal).

26

by Mokugyo

それとなく父は遺言状を書き

sore to naku chichi wa yuigonjyou wo kaki

no matter what—
father has already written
his final will*

---

* Literal: Nevertheless, father has gone and written out his will. Translation note: *Yuigon* means last will. The suffix *jyou* means terms or conditions. Contextual note: at this time (August 15) there were many rumors about incidents at the Tule Lake camp and the move from the Portland Assembly Center. People would have feared the worst, including death.

27

by Hikari

覚悟していながらもしやに望み持ち

kakugo shite i-nagara moshiya ni nozomi mochi

it is resolved
I accept what will be!
holding on to hope*

---

*Literal: Reaching acceptance on my part, yet I am still holding out hope. Translation note: *Kakugo* means resolution, acceptance; *I-nagara* means from where I sit, my point of view. *Ya* is an emphatic—similar to an exclamation point.

28

by Jōnan

覚悟して居ても移動に氣が参る

kakugo shite ite mo idou ni ki ga mairu

when transport begins
your resolute spirit—
may be overwhelmed*

---

*Literal: Even if you've made up your mind to be resolute—still the transfer (physical movement) might overwhelm your spirit (p. 16 of journal). Jonan may have made an error in the kanji. As near as we can tell, he intended to write *ki ga mairu* (氣が参る), which means one's spirit is overwhelmed, but used *on yomi* for rice (*mai*) in a phonetic transcription (氣が米る).

29

by Shousui

共
に
死
ぬ
覚
悟
四
千
里
こ
こ
へ
来
た

tomo ni shinu kakugo shi senri koko e kita

to live with you
a ten-thousand-mile trip
resigned to die with you*

---

* Literal: I came here 16,000 kilometers, just to be prepared to die with you. Translation note: *Kakugo*, or resignation, echoes no. 4, raising the possibility that this poem is written in reply to that one. *Ri* is an old Japanese measure of distance, approximately 3.9 km in length (rounded to miles). See "About the Translations" for a detailed discussion of the intentions behind this poem.

About Anything

August 22, 1942

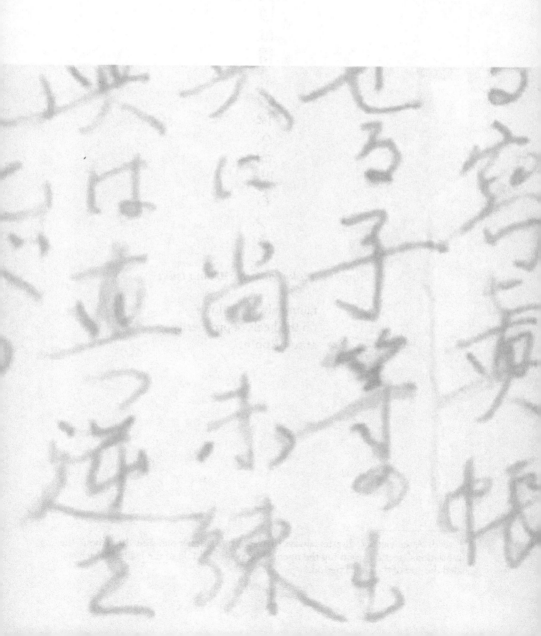

30

by Uson

失
敗
は
得
意
の
後
へ
何
時
も
つ
き

shippai wa tokui no ato e itsumo tsuki

failure always follows
on the heels of prosperity
at some point*

---

*Literal: After victory, disaster always arrives. Translation note: See the "About the Translations" section regarding the opening lines of the "Tale of the Heike," which signaled the end of the Heian period.

31

by Jōnan

対抗で初めて見せた師の妙技

tai kou de hajimete miseta shi no myougi

awestruck—
first time watching him
the master's fighting skills*

---

*Literal: In the contest (fight), first time I see the master's exquisite skill (p. 17 of the journal). Contextual note: Sumo wrestling demonstrations were held in the WCCA.

32

by Jōnan

無
料
で
見
る
活
動
に
さ
へ
不
平
あ
り

muryou de miru katsudou ni sae fuhei ari

their free movie—
such generosity
escapes me!*

---

*Literal: Even though the movie is free, this generosity does not satisfy me (p. 19 of journal).

33

by Goichi

平
和
ま
で
逢
え
ね
寫
眞
の
子
と
語
る

heiwa made aenu shashin no ko to kataru

only this photo can hold
the child we talk about—
until peace comes*

---

* Literal: We talk about this child in the photo, who we can't meet again until peace is declared. Translation note: The original poem does not say who the child in the photo is, but it's reasonable to assume it's a close relative. Contextual note: Incarcerated Issei parents were at times separated from their children because of the child's military service, attendance at school, or work in a state that was not in the military strategic areas along the Pacific Coast.

34

by Jōnan

寫眞では父も優しい美しい男

shashin de wa chichi mo yasashii yoi otoko

even father
handsome and light-hearted
in this picture*

---

*Literal: Father in the picture—easygoing beautiful man. Translation note: The characters for *shashin* (photograph) have been simplified since this poem was written (p. 19 of journal).

35

by Jōnan

嫌だわと逃げて其実撮らせる氣

'iya da wa' to nigete sono jitsu toraseru ki

picture request
coyly I ran away
but soon returned*

---

* Literal: I hated being in the picture, so I ran away—but in the end I let you take it.
Cultural note: Rinko Jeffers added that this is a typical behavior of a young girl who is pretending to be coy in regard to pictures (p. 20 of journal).

36

by Jōnan

旅に居る夫の寫眞へ話しかけ

tabi ni iru otto no shashin e hanashi kake

my husband left—
so now I talk to him
in his picture*

---

*I find myself talking to the picture of my husband—now that he has left (p. 20 of journal).

37

by Jōnan

アルバムへ幅を利かせる子等のもの

'arubamu' e haba wo kikaseru kora no mono

this album
is one where the kids take
all the spaces[*]

---

[*] Literal: In this album, the kids are taking possession of the space (p. 20 of journal).

38

by Jōnan

寫
眞
撮
る
娘
の
召
替
は
小
半
日

shashin toru ko no meshikae wa kohan niche

half the day spent
on a change of clothes—
her picture day*

---

* Literal: It's taking her half a day to change her clothes for the picture. Translation note: The characters for *shashin* (photograph) have been simplified since this poem was written (p. 20 of journal).

39

by Jōnan

母の髪寫眞に残る二〇三

haha no kami shashin ni nokoru 'ni-rei-san'

in the picture
mother's hairdo
like the "2-0-3" hill—*

---

* Literal: In the picture, all that is left of mother's hair is a "2-0-3" pattern. Translation note: The term "2-0-3" appears to refer to "203 Hill" near Dalian in China. In 1904, this hill, which was 203 meters above sea level, was the scene of a famous brutal and costly battle between the Japanese and the Russians in the Russo-Japanese War. It was memorialized in a Chinese poem "The Mountain Where Your Souls Lie" and achieved a notoriety similar to "Pork Chop Hill" in the Korean War. Jōnan is suggesting this hair style looks like a battle scene or possibly is piled high on her head (p. 22 of journal).

40

by Jōnan

初
聲
を
待
つ
間
母
親
落
付
か
ず

ubugoe wo matsuma haha-oya ochitsukazu

our mother too
anxiously listens
for baby's first cry*

---

*Literal: Mother is so excited waiting for baby's first cry, she can't calm down.
Translation note: The first two characters are normally pronounced *hatsugoe*, referring
to the first bird songs of spring, but more likely the author intended *ubugoe* (産聲),
the first cry of a newborn baby. The character for *goe* (*koe*) has since been simplified
to 声. The last *zu* is typically a negative particle, implying that things are not calming
down (p. 23 in journal). Contextual note: The birth announcement closest to this
date was published in the *Evacuazette* on August 18. The baby born was a boy to the
Okimoto family at 7:20 p.m. on August 15, 1942. Several babies were born during the
approximate three-month period at the WCCA Assembly Center.

41

by Jōnan

初聲に家中ホット安堵する

ubugoe ni iejyuu 'hotto' ando suru

the whole center
when the baby first cries
sighs of relief*

---

*Literal: Baby's first cry—warm with relief the entire house. Translation note: The first two characters are normally pronounced *hatsugoe*, referring to the first bird songs of spring, but more likely the author intended *ubugoe* (産聲), the first cry of a newborn baby. The character for *goe* (*koe*) has since been simplified to 声. *Hotto* in this poem is written in *katakana*, which indicates that the English word "hot" was implied (p. 24 of journal). In colloquial Japanese usage, it is also onomatopoeia for a sigh of relief (e.g., "whew!") (p. 24 of journal).

42

by Goichi

移
動
地
も
極
り
別
れ
る
日
が
せ
ま
り

idouchi mo kiwamari wakareru hi ga semari

decided now
my new destination—
our breakup is near[*]

---

[*] Literal: The place where I am to be moved has been determined, so the day of being parted approaches. Translation note: *Wakareru* is the passive voice to emphasize the parting is not voluntary. Contextual note: This may be referring to the breaking up of the Washington Japanese Americans from the Oregon Japanese Americans. Those from Oregon typically went to the Minidoka camp in Idaho, while those from Washington went to the Heart Mountain camp in Wyoming. The WCCA Assembly Center senryū group comprised poets from both states, and they may have known each other prior to their incarceration.

43

by Jōnan

炎天に投手はやけに汗を拭き

enten ni toshu wa yake ni ase wo fuki

hot summer day—
the pitcher wipes sweat
off his red face*

---

* Literal: Hot summer day—the pitcher wiping sweat off his hot face (p. 24 of journal).

44

by Jōnan

砂遊びボーイ矢張り意地を出し

suna asobi 'bo—i' yahari iji wo dashi

playing in sand
the little boy at last
is determined.*

---

*Literal: Little boy playing in the sand—at last he shows his determination. Translation note: *bo—i* is written in katakana, indicating the English word "boy."

45

by Jōnan

感激の涙で送るビーツ行き

kangeki no namida de okuru 'bi—tsu' iki

we see you off
through flowing tears
to the beet fields*

---

* Literal: Through tears of deep emotion—we see you off for the "beets." Translation note: *bi—tsu* is written in katakana (p. 25 of journal). See story about the Japanese Americans who volunteered to work in the beet fields of Idaho instead of continuing their stay at the WCCA center (in the Introduction).

46

by Jōnan

命
令
へ
秋
が
来
た
よ
な
収
合
所

meirei e aki ga kita yo na shuugousho

even autumn
comes on command here—
assembly center*

---

*Literal: Even fall comes on command at the assembly center (p. 25 of journal).

47

by Jōnan

センターで命名札もなつかしい

"senta—" de mei mei fuda mo natsukashii

someday after—
Center name cards just might
be nostalgic*

---

* Literal: After the center, even our name cards might someday become nostalgic (p. 25 of journal).

48

by Jōnan

夢
に
し
て
別
れ
る
に
チ
ト
未
練
あ
り

yume ni shite wakareruni 'chito' miren ari

dreams of leaving
and yet a little chip
clings to me[*]

---

[*] Literal: I dream of leaving this place, but somehow, I'm still a bit attached to it.
Translation note: *chito* is written in katakana. This may be a unique word created by the
incarcerated Japanese Americans or a foreign word or it could be a shortened version
of *notchit*. The collection of essays and personal accounts *Only What We Could Carry*,
by Lawson Inada (233), contains a glossary of words created by local Japanese. *Notchit*
is one of these words, which describes the little chip produced when a notch was made
on a two-by-five piece of wood to mark the days passed by in the concentration camps.
Alternatively, Rinko Jeffers suggests *chito* is a colloquial Japanese term for *chotto*, which
means a little chip.

49

by Jōnan

わきまへて居たに汽車場でホロリする

wakimaete ita ni kishaba de 'horori' suru

my self-control departs
at the train station
I'm moved to tears*

---

*Literal: No matter how controlled I try to be, I cry (every time) at the train station. Translation note: *horori* is written in katakana, as if to emphasize its impact. This is actually a Japanese word for being moved to tears (p. 25 of the journal).

50

by Shinsetsu

お馴染みとなってわかれるのも運命

o-najimi to natte wakareru no mo sadame

destiny determined
the honor of meeting you
and the sadness of parting*

---

*Literal: Like the honor to become acquainted with you (the sadness of) being parted is also fate. Translation note: *unmei* means fate, destiny; *o-najimi* is an honorific form of meeting, which may imply self-deprecation in addressing one considered older or superior in rank, or it may be a form of extreme politeness. Contextual note: Many of the detainees described the sadness of leaving new friends they met. Also, the Issei senryū poets knew of each other's senryū groups and individual poets. There was at least one well-known senryū poet at the assembly center.

51

by Choubou

もう逢えね覚悟で強く手を握り

mou aenu kakugo de tsuyoku te wo nigiri

accepting that
we may not meet again—
I grab tight your hand*

---

*Literal: Already resigned not to meet again, I grasp your hand firmly. Translation note: The phrase about squeezing the other's hand contains no subject. So, there is a certain ambiguity between "I hold your hand" and "we hold hands." Contextual note: This is another senryū reflecting the parting of friends moving to the incarceration camps in Idaho and Wyoming.

52

by Jōnan

縁あらば又会ひませうと手を握り

En araba mata aimashou to te wo nigiri

hands tightly clasped—
I pray our destiny is
to meet again*

---

*Literal: Firmly holding your hand, I pray that our destiny will be to meet again.
Translation note: The character for *ai* in *aimashou* has changed since this poem was written. The senryū journal reads *a hi ma se u* instead (p. 26 of journal).

Confusion

August 22, 1942

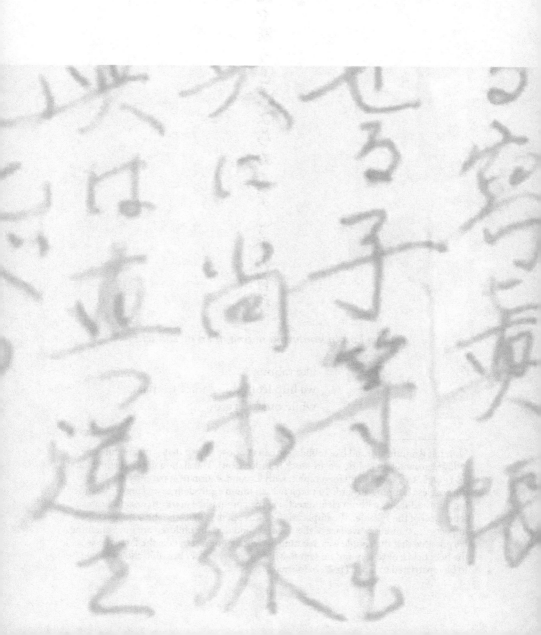

53

by Jōnan

兎や斯うと決まらぬままに子の育ち

to ya kou to kimaranu mama ni ko no sodachi

like rabbits
we hop from this choice to that
while our kids grow up*

---

*Literal: Running around like rabbits, we can't choose this or that—meanwhile our kids are growing up (while we are stuck in indecision). Translation note: The first kanji, 兎 (*usagi*, "to") is the kanji for a rabbit, with its connotation of apparently random, purposeless hopping around. *To yakou to* is an idiom equivalent to *arekore to*, meandering here and there, without clear direction. The comma-like mark after *ma* indicates a repetition of the syllable. The implication of this poem is that somehow the decision impacts the training or welfare of the children, and that the children are not benefiting. It's possible that the couple was debating on whether or not to take the family to work in the beet fields, or to stay and be sent to Minidoka, or another possible choice would be to be repatriated to Japan (p. 26 of journal).

54

by Kentsuku

迷から覚めて恥入る事ばかり

mayoi kara samete hajiiru koto bakari

having come to my senses
and abandoned delusion
I feel foolish*

---

* Literal: Awakening from confusion—only the feeling of embarrassment. Translation note: The kanji for *samete* (*sameru*), 覚, is a simplified form of the character in use since these poems were written.

55

by Jōnan

人生の迷路に立って未だ覚めず

jinsei no meiro ni tatte imada samezu

not awake yet
in this maze of life—
what is my path?*

---

*Literal: In the confusing labyrinth of life, I'm still not awake to what I should do (p. 26 of journal). Translation note: The kanji for *samezu* (*sameru*), 覚, is a simplified form of the character in use since these poems were written.

56

by Goichi

成行に任す心の静かなり

nariyuki ni makasu kokoro no shizuka nari

trusting events
to take their destined course
I will let it be so*

---

* Literal: My heart is at peace; I will let things take their course. Translation note: The phrase *nariyuki ni makasu* means allowing events to take their course. Contextual note: On August 19, 1942, the military announced the relocation plans to the Japanese Americans at the assembly center. Prior to the announcement, there was a great deal of worry and consternation regarding the move.

57

by Jōnan

迷
ひ
か
ら
覚
め
た
時
分
に
身
は
き
か
ず

mayoi kara sameta jibun ni mi wa kikazu

slow reactions
waking from confusion—
my body lingers*

---

*Literal: Waking up from my confusion (indecision), still unable to move quickly (decisively). Translation note: In the most literal terms, Jonan's poem reads "my body can't follow quickly" (p. 26 of journal). The kanji for *sameta* (*sameru*), 覚, is a simplified form of the character in use since these poems were written.

58

by Roshyou

永住も帰国も着かず日が過ぎる

eijuu mo kikoku mo tsukazu hi ga sugiru

stay forever or return home
my decision never made
too much to bear*

---

*Literal: Whether we stay forever or return home, it's too much that this decision is
never made. Translation note: *Tsukazu* is a poetic negation of *tsuku* (to arrive). *Sugiru*
means "too much" or excessive. The first kanji in *kikoku* (*kaeru*), 歸, has been simplified
to 帰 since these poems were written. Contextual note: This has to do with repatriation.
While at the center, Issei or Nisei with dual citizenship could voluntarily fill out a form
requesting to be repatriated to Japan. The form was made available on July 21, 1942, and
had to be returned by July 24, 1942.

Doubt

August 22, 1942

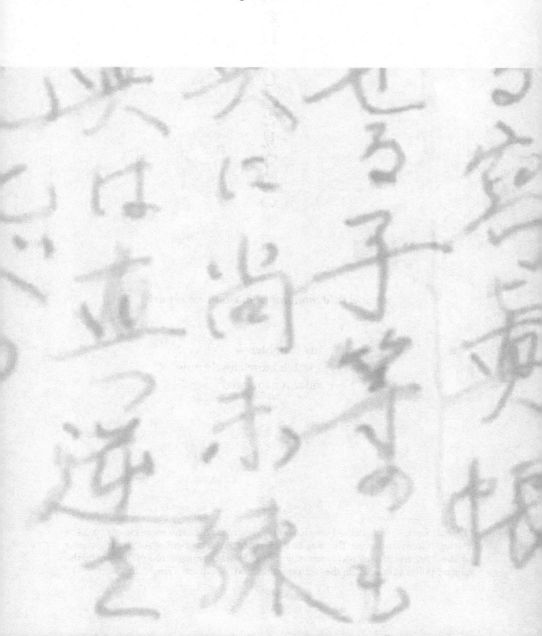

59

by Jōnan

あれ以来じっと見守娘の素振り

are irai jitto mimamoru musume no soburi

my daughter—
I watch more closely now
since it happened*

---

*Literal: Since it happened—I watch over my daughter's behavior more closely (p. 28 of journal). Contextual note: This may be a reference to the incident of August 15, when a Japanese American cook was reportedly shot as he was coming through the gate by the military police (discussed in the "Introduction" and "About the Translations" sections).

60

by Jōnan

疑
へ
ば
限
り
な
き
世
を
清
く
活
き

utagaeba kagiri naki yo wo kiyoku iki

reasons for doubts
everywhere—just stay focused
on the world you see*

---

* Literal: Opportunities for doubt are all around, with no limits, the remedy is to focus purely on the world (*yo*) in front of you—to stay "present in the moment." Translation note: The handwritten character for *yo* cannot be found. It may be an error (p. 28 of journal).

61

by Jōnan

此
の
頃
の
妻
の
そ
ぶ
り
が
腑
に
落
ち
ず

kono goro no tsuma no soburi ga fu ni ochizu

these days
my wife's behaviors
make me queasy*

---

*Literal: My wife's behavior these days—doesn't feel quite right. Translation note: *Fu niochiru*—to settle in the stomach, feel right. The *zu* particle in *ochizu* negates the meaning—this behavior won't settle in the stomach, doesn't feel right (p. 29 of journal).

62

by Jōnan

絶
交
の
友
へ
も
し
か
と
思
ふ
節

zekko no tomo e moshika to omou fushi

our friendship is broken
but something tells me
perhaps . . .*

---

* Literal: This estrangement with my friend—can something be done I wonder? (p. 29 of journal).

63

by Jōnan

疑
ひ
も
晴
れ
て
甦
生
國
の
た
め

utagai mo harete kousei kuni no tame

cleared of suspicion
I will start a new life
for the sake of this country*

---

*Literal: Cleared of suspicion—I will be reborn for my country. Translation note:
Jōnan is perhaps looking forward to the day when the incarceration is over, and he is
vindicated (p. 29 of the journal).

64

by Mokugyo

手間取ったわけが何だか腑に落ちず

tema dotta wake ga nandaka fu ni ochizu

still more delays?
no matter the reasons
I can't stomach it*

---

* Literal: More unexpected delays? Whatever the reason, this doesn't sit well in my stomach. Translation note: *Tema* means difficulties, travails. *Dotta* means to have encountered these difficulties (in making the decision). The term *wake* indicates that the delays are the reason for what follows, meaning an expression of dissatisfaction. *Funiochizu* literally means not to fall into the gut—that is, the delays do not fall well into my stomach, and cause my gut to be unsettled. Contextual note: This again has to do with the last couple of weeks at the center, with the unknowns about when the move will take place and where the locations will be.

65

by Kentsuku

汽車が出る迄を淋しく笑ひ合ひ

kisha ga deru made wo sabishiku warai ai

melancholy laughter
help us pass the time
until the train departs[*]

---

[*] The train was departing to the Minidoka Idaho incarceration camp between August and September (p. 22 of journal).

66

by Kahō

わがままを許してくれたありがたさ

wagamama wo yurushite kureta arigatasa

forgiven
for my insistence—
so grateful*

---

* Literal: You were so kind to forgive me doing it my way—so grateful. Translation note: The expression *waga mama* literally means "my way" but carries overtones of selfishness and stubbornness. It is often used as a general description of an individual's character.

67

by Sen Taro

疑ひのあるなし問はず収容し

utagai no aru nashi towazu shuuyoushi

they never asked
suspicious or not—
just put us away*

---

* Literal: Suspicious or not, they never asked—just put us away (a cynical reminder that justice had nothing to do with the original decision to detain them) (p. 29 of journal). Translation note: The second character of *towazu* (は) is likely an error. It should be わ. The former is pronounced *wa* only when used as a particle indicating sentence topic, while the latter is the standard hiragana for *wa* when embedded in a word.

一九四四年一月 浅間
「感謝纂詠集」

HOLLAND LINEN

FINISH

SENRYU — JAN. — 1944

No. I.

Japanese American World War II soldier on a pillar at the Japanese American Historical Plaza and Bill of Rights Memorial in Portland, Oregon. Photo credit: Shelley Baker-Gard

Afterword

After World War II, many of the poets incarcerated at the Portland Wartime Civilian Control Administration (WCCA) Assembly Center, and at Minidoka, Idaho; Tule Lake, California; and Heart Mountain, Wyoming, returned to their west coast home states, and some chose to move to other states. The recovery and rebuilding of the community took many years to occur. It was not until August 1988 that the US Congress passed the HR442 legislation, which acknowledged the government's error in the World War II treatment of our Japanese American citizens and allowed for $20,000 in reparation payments to any surviving Japanese American who was incarcerated. The first payments were distributed in 1990 at a Washington, DC, ceremony.

On August 3, 1990, the cherry-tree-lined Japanese American Historical Plaza and Bill of Rights Memorial was opened in Portland, Oregon, to help tell the story of the Japanese immigrants to America and their contributions to our country. It also memorializes the Japanese American soldiers who bravely fought during World War II and reminds visitors of the Bill of Rights, which was violated by the forced removal of Japanese Americans from their homes. The plaza was created through the efforts of the Oregon Nikkei Endowment in Portland, Oregon, and the help they received from various City of Portland government agencies and funding support from many Northwest corporations.[*]

Another memorial was created in 2004 at the Portland Expo Center. There the Portland artist Valerie Otani designed and placed tall torii gates titled *Voices of Remembrance* at the Max Transit station stop. High from each gate dangle silver tags that hold the names of each family member held at the WCCA Assembly Center. Engraved on the supporting poles are newspaper articles describing the Evacuation Order and the families leaving their homes. These gates provide a powerful reminder of an event that should never happen again.

The editors of this anthology sincerely hope the poems in it will also shed light on the struggles and perseverance of the Japanese Americans

---

[*] For further information, see http://www.oregonnikkei.org/plaza.htm.

Above: Torii Gates, an installation piece in Voices of Remembrance, by Portland artist Valerie Otani at the Portland Expo Center, which includes the names of all the Japanese Americans incarcerated at the assembly center at this location. Photo credit: Shelley Baker-Gard

Below left: Engraving of a Japanese American woman created from a picture in a 1942 Oregonian newspaper article that appears on one of the pillars of the Torii Gates. Photo credit: Shelley Baker-Gard

Below right: Engraving on Expo Center Torii Gate Pillar of newspaper headline, May 1942. Photo credit: Mike Freiling

and that we never forget their contributions to our country. The following poems are engraved in Japanese script on twelve granite stones at the Japanese American Historical Plaza; their translations appear below. All of the poets were incarcerated at the Portland WCCA Assembly Center.

by Lawson Fusao Inada

Just over there
was our old community
Echoes! Echoes! Echoes!

With new hope
we build new lives
why complain when it rains?
this is what it means to be free.

Mighty Willamette!
Beautiful friend
I am learning
I am practicing
to say your name.
Sure, I go to school
Same as you
I'm an American.

Who?
What?
When?
Where?
Why?

by Shizue Iwatsuki

War and change
My native land
Once so hard to leave
is behind me now
forever.

Glancing up
At red tinged mountains
My heart is softened
A day in deep Autumn

Through the car window
a glimpse of pines
Oregon Mountains
My heart beats faster
returning home.

Going home
Feeling cheated
Gripping my daughter's hand
without emotion

Black smoke rolls
Across the blue sky
Winter chills our bones
This is Minidoka

Our young men and women
joined the army too.
They are proud to be American.

by Hisako Saito (Ryūko)

Breathe the Japanese
Of Japan and America
In the city of Roses

Hisako Saito's senryū on a granite memorial stone at the Japanese
American Historical Plaza in downtown Portland. Photo credit:
Shelley Baker-Gard

by Masaki Kinoshita (Jōnan)

Footprints of 100 years
Trace the history
Of Japanese Americans

Mataksi Kinoshita's senryū on a granite memorial stone at the Japanese American Historical Plaza in downtown Portland. Photo credit: Duane Watari, 2020

Reflections on First-Person Experience in War Haiku

FAY AOYAGI

息白く唄ふガス室までの距離堀田季何

iki shiroku utau gasu-shitsu made no kyori

singing in white breath
the distance
to a gas chamber

少年少女焚火す銃を組立てつつ堀田季何

shounen shoujo takibi su juu o kumitatetsutsu

boys and girls
make a bonfire
assembling guns

by Kika Hotta

These haiku are included in Kika Hotta's haiku collection, which was published in 2021.[1] In the afterword, he states, "I wrote about the human actions in the period I was not born," and the "[I] in some of this haiku is not the poet himself, but a human personality from either the past or the future." The collection received acclaim from prominent haiku poets and critics in Japan.

I believe haiku, as in these examples, can be socially conscious and express things we did not personally experience. A question that arises is how we use experiences we did not have.

なまなまと白紙の遺髪秋の風飯田蛇笏

namanama to hakushi no ihatsuaki no kaze

the hair of the deceased
on the vivid white paper
autumn wind

by Dakotsu Iida[2]

After I read Hotta's collection, the above haiku by Dakotsu Iida came to my mind. He lost his eldest son in the Battle of Leyte Gulf during World War II. Many surviving families in Japan at this time received only a lock of their hair after their loved ones' deaths. Though I've never experienced war, I can visualize what Iida wrote. It makes me feel as if I am in the poem, experiencing it for myself. My father told me when his older brother died during World War II, his family didn't receive anything other than an official notice of his death.

Tet:
Both armies
Wet

by Ty Hadman[3]

This poem is based on Hadman's own Vietnam War experiences. When Americans fought in Vietnam, I was in Tokyo. I had no American friends. I did not imagine I would be a naturalized American citizen one day. The Vietnam War was a "foreign" war to me. Then, why am I attracted to Hadman's Vietnam war haiku? I was born in 1956. I belong to the same generation as Americans who were drafted. If I were Vietnamese, I could have been one of the refugees who fled the country by boat. Perhaps that is why Hadman's haiku speaks to me. I became more interested in the Vietnam War after I moved to the United States and read *A Prayer for Owen Meany* by John Irving. More recently, I've read books by Vietnamese American authors, such as Vu Tran, Viet Than Nguyen, and Eric Nguyen. Maybe I try to understand more about the Vietnam War now because I am a "hyphenated" American.

Holocaust Museum
in every photo
my family

by Carolyn Hall[4]

There is a strong sentiment in Carolyn Hall's haiku. We are all humans. We may call other human beings "family," despite their colors of skins, eyes, and hair. But I am not Jewish like Hall, and I will not see "my" family. When I was a child, I read a Japanese translation of *The Diary of a Young Girl* by Anne Frank. I learned about the Holocaust at school and watched movies and documentaries. I even visited the famous attic, now the Anne Frank Museum, in Amsterdam. Have I tried to write about the Holocaust? I guess the answer is no. It was a human tragedy. You don't have to be Jewish to condemn the horrifying act. Despite this, because of something deep inside of me, I don't think I am qualified to write about it.

In the Imperial Japanese Army, Unit 731 was in charge of biological and chemical warfare development and research. It was based in

Harbin, Manchukuo, the Japanese puppet state in northern China. Doctors and researchers from prominent universities in Japan performed human experiments on local Chinese people. Examinees were disparagingly called *maruta* (a log). I don't have any family members—even distant relatives—who belonged to this devilish unit. Still, I cannot shake the idea of having an aggressor's blood because of my ancestry. On the other hand, I come from the country where atomic bombs were dropped twice, and so can say I have "victim's" blood as well. In spite of feeling this way, I am not saying people have to inherit the sins of their ancestors or play the role of victim by proxy.

Pigs cannot fly in the real world, yet we can imagine how we would feel if we were given wings or fins. We can act as a sniper, a bomber, or a submarine operator in our poems. We are in the "progressive" twenty-first century. An African American actor can play Hamlet at the theater. An Asian American actor can be a Superman or Wonder Woman in the movie. Metaphorically, I can ride on the back of Hiroshige's hawk, or apply to become a crab, in haiku. Even so, I have not been able to put myself in the shoes of a Holocaust victim. Though I grew up in an ethnically homogeneous Japan, I have spent more than a half of my life in the United States, which is now my adopted country. I write haiku in English, my second language. There are people around me with many different backgrounds and ethnicities. I am not very political, but aware of international issues, as well as domestic ones. I have written some Hiroshima haiku. I picked up Japanese incarceration camps as a theme before. Why do I feel I cannot write from the point of view of a Holocaust victim? Is it because it happened in Europe? Is it because I belong to a different race? Is it because I feel there might be more "suitable" people than me? I can't say for sure.

I grew up in an old Japanese-style house. There was a long external corridor. It had no sliding glass doors along it, and we had to close wood storm shutters after sunset. It looked like a long dark hole. I can visualize the image Watanabe (1913–1969) presents. I feel the poet's fear. Something terrible like war should not enter one's house, which is supposed to be a safe harbor. Watanabe's haiku is categorized as *juugo haiku* (home-front haiku). During World War II, various cities in Japan and Europe were bombed. Many civilians lost their lives. You don't have to be Japanese to understand this haiku. War changes everyone's life.

戦争が廊下の奥に立つてゐた渡辺白泉

sensou ga rouka no oku ni tatte ita

deep in the corridor war was standing

by Hakusen Watanabe[5]

In the *New York Times*, I read an article about an Afghan woman who fled her country with her husband, with just one backpack. She was pregnant and gave birth at the refugee camp. You may have read or watched similar stories. As haiku poets, should we spread a story like hers? News footage on TV gives us a powerful image. Can we digest it and compose strong haiku? Can we move a reader even though we sit comfortably at home, away from bombshells? I think that we can try. On February 24, 2022, Russia invaded Ukraine. San Francisco, where I live, has many Russian and Ukrainian descendants. The area called "Russian Hill" is in my neighborhood. Is that enough for me to compose on a tragedy happening in Europe? Will I be able to create a convincing *juugo haiku*?

Hotta's haiku threw a very big stone into my mind's well. Everyone can write about war—even without experiencing it firsthand. What is the difference between "authentic" haiku and "didactic" haiku? How can we avoid writing journalistic photographic haiku? Honestly, I don't know the answer.

spring chill
a crow perched on
war

by Fay Aoyagi

Fay Aoyagi was born in Tokyo and now lives in San Francisco. She started writing haiku in English in 1995 and later started writing it in Japanese, too. She has published three books: Chrysanthemum Love, In Borrowed Shoes, *and* Beyond the Reach of My Chopsticks. *She is a former president of the Haiku Society of America and is an associate editor of the* Heron's Nest *journal. This essay was originally published in the Haiku Society of America online newsletter, March 2022, https://www.hsa-haiku.org/newsletter.htm.*

American English Senryū and Haiku

Knowledge of Japanese poetry seeped into the Western world at the end of the nineteenth century. The earliest publications on Japanese poetics were written by Basil Hall Chamberlain (1850–1935), a British citizen and scholar of Japanese culture who taught in Tokyo until 1892.[1] In 1880, he published *Classical Poetry of the Japanese*; in 1902, in the journal *Transactions of the Asiatic Society of Japan*, he published the article, "Bashō and the Japanese Poetical Epigram." What Chamberlain called an "epigram" was later called a *hokku* and then, in English, a "haiku."

Sadakichi Hartmann (1867–1944) was another early advocate of writing Japanese poetry forms in English. He was a Japanese German American (1867–1944), born in Japan to a Japanese mother and a German (Prussian) merchant. His mother died when he was an infant, and he spent his childhood in Europe. Sadakichi came to the United States in 1882 and became a citizen in 1892. In addition to being a poet, Sadakichi was well known as a critic of art and photography.[2] In 1904, he wrote an important article in *The Reader* magazine, "The Japanese Conception of Poetry." In the article, he provided an overview of the Japanese poetry forms and Japanese aesthetics for English speakers. He wrote that Japanese poetry is a "unison of the external beauties of nature and the subtleties of the human soul."[3] In 1916, Hartmann self-published a collection of Japanese poetry forms in English titled *Japanese Rhythms* (expanded in 1933).[4] In the 1933 version, he includes his own tanka and haiku poems in addition to his English translations of several Japanese poets' *hokku* (haiku), including Bashō's famous depiction of a crow sitting on a tree branch during an autumn sunset.

The month after Sadakichi Hartmann wrote his article, the Japanese poet, literary critic, and novelist Yone Noguchi (1875–1947) wrote a follow-up article in *The Reader*, "A Proposal to American Poets."[5] In it, Noguchi encouraged "long winded English speaking poets": "Pray, you try Japanese *hokku*, my American Poets!" He provided multiple examples of his own *hokku* (haiku) in English. Both Noguchi and Hartmann knew Walt Whitman and many of the Imagist poets of their time. Noguchi returned to Japan in 1904, and during World War II, he became a sympathizer to the nationalist government of Japan. His home in Tokyo was destroyed by American firebombing in 1945.[6]

The composing of haiku in the United States by native English speakers began around 1913, when Imagist poet Ezra Pound wrote a two-line poem, "In a Station at the Metro" using a haiku-like style.[7] Pound described his style in the March 1913 *Poetry* magazine essay, "A Few Don'ts by an Imagiste," as "that which presents an intellectual and emotional complex in an instant of time."[8] Interest in composing haiku among American English poets increased progressively with each decad as Japanese haiku translations were published. The following authors and their critical analysis of Japanese poetry forms are considered highly influential in spreading the popularity of English language haiku.

In 1933, Japanese translator and Asian academic Harold G. Henderson published a small volume of Japanese haiku called the *Bamboo Broom*, which he translated into English using a rhyme scheme of a-b-a. He felt that even though haiku in Japanese were never rhymed, the rhyme did provide an image frame to the English translation.[9] In 1940, Asataro Miyamori published a revised edition of his book *Haiku Poems, Ancient and Modern*. In it, he included a section with examples of writing haiku in English.[10] Harold G. Henderson was a contemporary and friend to the Asian historian, haiku theorist, and translator R. H Blyth, with whom he corresponded frequently.[11] Blyth's publications over the decades have become seminal texts of nearly biblical proportion and likely sit on the shelves of many haiku and senryū poets throughout the world.

After World War II, in 1949, R. H. Blyth wrote the first of his four-volume series on haiku, which heavily focused on the influence of Zen Buddhism especially in the classical Japanese *hokku* of Matsuo Bashō.[12] Since Bashō's time (1644–1694), the traditional Japanese haiku has often exhibited aesthetics found in Zen Buddhism and the Shinto religious views, which seek harmony between humans and the *kami* spirits that inhabit all living things.[13]

The Japanese cultural aesthetics of *wabi* and *sabi*, often paired together as *wabi sabi,* especially in the English-speaking world, have ambiguous and culturally imbedded meanings that have evolved over centuries and suggest impermanence, humility, asymmetry, and the beauty of imperfection. These themes link them to a Zen Buddhist perspective, including the acceptance of the transient nature of all things.[14] Taken individually, *sabi* is associated with a sense of deep nostalgia, an appreciation of the passage of time, pathos, and the rhythms of life. Here is a poem by Matsuo Bashō, translated by Jane Reichhold, which she believes exhibits a sense of *sabi*.[15]

> dreaming of rice cakes
> fastened to folded ferns
> a grass pillow

The term *wabi* is generally described in English as a sense of beauty with austerity and forlorn aloneness. This poem by Bashō, also translated by Reichhold, has a feeling of *wabi*.[16]

> hibiscus flower
> naked I wear one
> in my hair

Without doubt, the aesthetics of *wabi* and *sabi* have meanings that are difficult to culturally translate into words, but in both English and Japanese haiku and senryū, they are felt on an emotional level.

Other less well-known Japanese aesthetics can appear in both Japanese and English haiku and senryū. Two of these are *yūgen* and *karumi*. *Yūgen* is defined in English as the sense of mystery in common things that cannot be fully understood. Yūgen has been described as integral to Japanese *nō* plays, where mystery can be evoked by the person behind a fan.[17] Here is one of Jane Reichhold's English poems she imbued with *yūgen*.[18]

> a swinging gate
> on both sides flowers
> open—close

Karumi in English means "lightness" and, according to Jane Reichhold, is a concept Bashō ascribed to late in his career in order to create haiku with fewer emotions. In Reichhold's translation, *karumi* gives this Bashō haiku a list-like appearance.[19]

> under the trees
> soup and pickles
> cherry blossoms

The Japanese idea of *ma* is another important concept, which emphasizes the contemplation of blank space. *Ma* space is noticed in sumi paintings, ikebana flower arrangements, the pause between musical notes, and what is left unsaid in a senryū or haiku.[20] The use of space is particularly notable in the artwork of the famous Chinese painter Ma Yüan, who lived during the Chinese Song Dynasty period known as the Southern Song (1127–1279). He was called "one corner Ma" as he would render most of the landscape painting as blank space, suggesting a sense of endlessness, and paint the rest of the scene in one corner.[21] Ma Yuan's work influenced the Japanese artist and Zen Buddhist monk Tensho Shubun (1380?–1444?), whose paintings also effectively used empty space in his landscapes. Acknowledging the "space" of what is left "unsaid" in a haiku is an important aspect of understanding this genre.

When World War II was over and the Tule Lake incarceration camp was closed, Kenneth Yasuda, who had been there, was able to resume his college studies. Yasuda earned his doctorate in 1955; his dissertation was on Japanese poetry forms. In 1957, he used his dissertation research to publish one of the first guides to writing haiku in English, *The Japanese Haiku: Its Essential Nature, History and Possibilities in English*.[22] In the sections on writing haiku in English, Yasuda suggested using a three-line 5-7-5 English syllable count form, as it matched the 5-7-5 *on* sound unit count of Japanese, and more importantly, a syllable count of sixteen to eighteen was the length of a poem that one could recite in the space of time of "one breath."[23] He also emphasized three attributes of a haiku that told the story of the experience the poet was relating in the poem: the when, where, and what.

Yasuda explains that the "when" part of the haiku, "is an aesthetic symbol of the sense of the seasons, arising from the oneness of man and nature, and its function is to symbolize this union."[24] The "where" can be a physical place, such as "on the branch"; it can be a "psychic location—such as a scene between lovers," or an imagined or implied place, such as a garden. The "what" is the point of the story. Yasuda states, "The common pattern of experience . . . is always in interaction between a live creature and some aspect of his environment." He quotes Isoji Asō, "grasping an insight into an object is accompanied by the feeling arising from it." According to Yasuda, this particular insight and feeling are what makes haiku unique in the world of poetry.[25] Yasuda was an advocate for both the use of rhythm (syllable count ratios per line "measure") and rhyme in translations. In American English haiku, he felt that rhyme, if used carefully and not forced, enhanced the aural depth of the haiku.[26]

Another contemporary of Henderson, Blyth, and Yasuda was the somewhat controversial Australian poet, Asian scholar, and devout Shin Buddhist Harold Stewart (1917–1995). Stewart felt that because there is a juxtaposition of two parts to a haiku, and because of the lyrical sound of the haiku when spoken in Japanese, they should be translated into a rhyming couplet.[27] His publications of translations of classic Japanese haiku, *A Net of Fireflies: Haiku and Haiga* and *A Chime of Windbells: A Year of Japanese Haiku in English*, are beautiful anthologies. Their beauty is due in part to the charming Japanese *haiga*, which in his books are *sumi* sketches accompanying the haiku. The books were wildly popular among the American public in the 1960s and were frequently given as gifts (as of this writing, *A Net of Fireflies* is in its twelfth printing).[28] Harold Stewart's publications undoubtably increased the interest in haiku, even though the couplet form never gained a following as it tended to close the poem for interpretation and insightful meaning. Interestingly, in 2013, Charles Trumbull discovered that Stewart included his own haiku in his publications under the penname Hô-ô (a mythical Japanese phoenix).

Another haiku scholar, the British American poet and composer Dorothy Britton (1922–2015) was born in Japan and was bilingual. In 1974, she translated Matsuo Bashō's travelogue about his journey to the northern province of Aomori (previously known as Michinoku). Like Henderson, Yasuda, and Stewart, she also used rhyme in her translations. For her, rhyme provided a sense of formality (reflecting the Japanese diction) to the haiku that she did not feel was adequately portrayed in a translation to free verse.[29]

However, Blyth's translations followed a fixed form of 5-7-5 syllable line count, and he felt this adequately provided, through syllable stresses, a lyrical sense. He believed a use of end rhyme tended to close the poem to multiple meanings.[30] In the end, Blyth's viewpoint on rhyme prevailed, and it is now rare to see an American English haiku with an end rhyme published. However, alliteration, consonance, and assonance are still employed, albeit judiciously.

Historically, in Western poetry, rhyme served the practical purpose of aiding in the memorization and recitation of the poem, but the one-breath length of haiku makes it easily remembered. Besides rhyme, there are other debated composition issues. One is whether or not to use punctuation as a replacement for a Japanese *kireji* (a cutting word) as an attempt to provide an indication of a line break, a pause, or an emphasis of an emotion, somewhat similar to what an exclamation point or dash does in English.[31] For a list and detailed explanation of cutting words, see the appendix in Henderson's guidebook, *Haiku in English*. Other issues discussed by Henderson are the number of lines needed for the poem and the number of English syllables to be counted or not counted (described in more detail below).

As a response to the many Americans reading about haiku and attempting to write it, in 1967 Harold G. Henderson published *Haiku in English*. This short volume is a concise how-to for writing and teaching haiku in English.[32] It quickly became a classic, and his suggestions are used in current times by many American haiku poets. In his conclusion, he states, "The vast majority of haiku in English, whatever their form, do treat nature, or some aspect of nature, as an integral part of the poem. Most express an emotion aroused by some one particular event and try to convey it to the reader as simply as possible."[33] In his guidebook, Henderson clearly explains the issues of equating the Japanese haiku form of 5-7-5 *on* sound units to English syllables, as the *on* sound unit is shorter in general than an English syllable. However, because early translators of Japanese haiku into English (including Henderson's) used a 5-7-5 English syllable form, American poets for many years considered it a required format. This, too, was frequently the way elementary school teachers taught students how to write haiku.

From the time of Henderson's 1967 guidebook to recent times, many other excellent how-to guides on writing haiku in English have been written, such as those by William J. Higginson with Penny Harter, Jane Reichhold, and Lee Gurga. Currently, many American poets do not compose haiku or senryū with a 5-7-5 syllable count form, primarily because it becomes a longer-sounding poem than a haiku in Japanese. As a result, most published American English haiku are seen with fewer than seventeen syllables and are often in a short-long-short three-line format. There is no consensus on how many syllables (stressed and or unstressed) should be used for a haiku form, and haiku can be composed with a one-, two-, and even four-line structure.

Additionally, some American English haiku groups understand the importance of form and ritual in general in Japanese traditions (such as a tea ceremony and ikebana flower arranging) and continue to write haiku with a 5-7-5 English syllable line pattern as one way to acknowledge this. The Yuki Teikei Haiku Society is one of these groups, and they hold an annual Tokutomi Memorial contest. The Buddhist magazine *Tricycle* also prefers haiku with a season word and a 5-7-5 syllable count. Another motivation for a set syllable count is it can be an entertaining challenge for some poets to keep a 5-7-5 structure. One way certain haiku and senryū poets have developed a solution to this issue is to write the poem in a 4-6-4, or 3-5-3 syllable line count form, or a 2-3-2 stressed syllable count. These changes may make the length more in tune to the 5-7-5 sound unit count of the traditional Japanese haiku. Patricia Machmiller provided an excellent overview of the options for writing haiku in a specific form and the corresponding syllable count in a 2002 article in the *Frogpond* journal.[34]

During the 1960s and into current times, some haiku and senryū poets experimented with "concrete" poetry and called their poems "haiku." Concrete poetry, also known as visual poetry, has ancient origins and relies in part on the way the words of the poem are arranged on the material or paper it is written on for its meaning.[35] If these poems are called haiku or senryū, and not simply "short concrete poems," then, because of their visual dependency, they perhaps are more akin to American English *haiga* than to American English haiku (*haiga* is a work of art accompanied by a poem. Taniguchi Buson (1715–1783) was a famous Japanese poet who excelled in the *haiga* form).

One well-known example of a visual haiku is Cor van den Heuvel's poem "tundra," which is just the word "tundra" in the middle of a white paper with the blank space (*ma*) providing the sense of the tundra.[36] This poem is reminiscent of the artwork of the Chinese painter Ma Yūen, who left his panel blank except for the scene painted in a corner.

The problem with most of the minimalist concrete haiku is that they cannot be recited or heard in a way that delivers the full meaning to the audience—saying "tundra" without its visual white space canvas would not do justice to this ingenious art poem. After all, haiku and senryū are poems that can be *spoken* in one breath.

As Henderson mentions, when deciding on what criteria is used in American English haiku, "the final decision rests with the poets themselves."[37] Nonetheless, since many poets want to be published, they are likely to also pay attention to what editors of journals think the criteria should be for a haiku. Two definitions of English haiku have been proposed by two prominent print journals published in the United States. The Haiku Society of America (HSA), which publishes the journal *Frogpond* and a yearly anthology, proposes, "A haiku is a short poem that uses imagistic language to convey the essence of an experience of nature or the season intuitively linked to the human condition."[38] HSA also notes,

Many so-called "haiku" in English are really senryū. Others, such as "spam-ku" and "headline haiku," seem like recent additions to an old Japanese category, *zappai*, miscellaneous amusements in doggerel verse (usually written in 5-7-5) with little or no literary value. Some call the products of these recent fads "pseudo haiku" to make clear that they are not haiku at all. [39]

From the journal *Modern Haiku,* the definition of haiku is

Haiku is a brief verse that epitomizes a single moment. It uses the juxtaposition of two concrete images, often a universal condition of nature and a particular aspect of human experience, in a way that prompts the reader to make an insightful connection between the two. The best haiku allude to the appropriate season of the year. Good haiku avoid subjectivity; intrusions of the poet's ego, views, or values; and displays of intellect, wit, and facility with words.

The *Modern Haiku* editors add, "The above is a *normative* definition, and haiku of various kinds not squaring with this definition can be easily found, even in the pages of our journal."[40]

In 1999, at an international haiku convention in Japan, a group of prominent haiku scholars and poets—Arima Akito, Haga Tōru, Ueda Makoto, Soh Sakon, Kaneko Tohta, and Jean Jacques Origas—delivered the "Matsuyama Declaration."[41] They announced the establishment of a Masaoka Shiki International Haiku Research Center in Matsuyama, Japan, where Masaoka Shiki lived (the founding father of the modern haiku in the last part of the nineteenth century). In their declaration, they acknowledged and advocated for the spread of haiku as a poetry form throughout the world. They noted the difficulties in transferring the structure of haiku to other languages and cultures, because of its inextricable link to Japanese cultural traditions and language. Yet, they firmly believed these difficulties could be resolved through the internationalization of haiku and dialogue with poets all over the world. The following quotes are just a few points they emphasized as haiku guidelines in the declaration.

[From section 6] In haiku we find the special quality of rising above the self-awareness of the Western-type modern individualism and reaching a realm where we connect ourselves with nature. . . . Haiku and nature are one and the same. Perhaps haiku, nature and people all share the cycle of life, death, and rebirth. Therefore, when we talk about the destruction of the natural environment, we should not regard ourselves as protecting nature, but cultivate the awareness of being a part of nature. Since this is the basic characteristic of haiku, it will have an important role in environmental issues. . . . With the rapid destruction of the natural environment these days, the act of composing haiku gives a perfect opportunity to reconsider the relationship between people and nature. We look to the various poetries of the world to give us the power to heal people's anguish, to recover harmony and return to a symbiotic relationship with nature.

In section 4, they speak to *teikei*, the fixed 5-7-5 *on* sound unit form in Japanese: "The 5-7-5 rhythm is unique to the Japanese language. . . . *Teikei* is not about the matter of syllable count or accent, but the matter of the way poetic expression could be heightened through tension when the writer wants it." They also discuss *kigo*, which in Japanese haiku are season words that have a contextual history associated with them in addition to the time of the year (to say "cherry blossom" also indicates spring and the festivals for viewing them). For the non-Japanese poet, they state, "It is extremely important to describe nature by perceiving the relationship between nature and human beings based on the haiku insight, it doesn't necessarily have to be in the form of *kigo*. In other words, when we discuss haiku from a global perspective, the contents of haiku will have a closer relation with each country's local characteristics. . . . It is a keyword that possesses a symbolic meaning unique to that particular culture." [42]

There are now hundreds of haiku poets in the United States, and currently there is no unified agreement on the form or criteria for a haiku—but in general, most poems do follow the definitions as laid out by the HSA and the *Modern Haiku* journal. However, a significant minority of poems published as a modern haiku in the United States have no perceived criteria or fixed form (other than they are short). Jim Kacian describes this diversity well in a *Frogpond* essay. In it, he indicates American English haiku can be seen as a reflection of the US values of individualism, innovation, and progress. Individualism is expressed when the poet picks the structure and tradition to follow or not to follow when composing the poem. Innovation is a value reflected in the ideology that "new is better" and progress is innovation that leads to the "advancement of the genre." He states "Most haiku fall into one of two categories, either the one-line monoku or the three-line haiku. However, the variety to be discovered in these categories is astounding."[43] Not all haiku poets in the United States hold these values to be particularly important, especially if they believe that what is most valued in their haiku is an image that reflects a "symbiotic relationship with nature."[44] Consequently, this lack of consensus on what constitutes a short poem's membership in the genre of haiku can be a controversial subject for the American English haiku poet community.

Many of the American English haiku poets also write senryū, which in English seldom follows a 5-7-5 syllable count (while many poets state they write both haiku and senryū in American English, many do not distinguish their poems as one or the other and simply give both types a generic "haiku" classification). By contrast, in Japanese, the *on* sound unit count for the senryū-like haiku is most frequently in a 5-7-5 *on* pattern. The senryū genre is focused primarily on human-to-human interactions and doesn't require a seasonal or nature reference.

Historically, senryū was not paid nearly same the attention that haiku was in its introduction to US English poets. However, R. H. Blyth did write three books specifically on senryū and satirical verse of Japan (1949, 1961, 1971). After haiku became popular in the United States, many poets wrote haiku that were actually senryū.[45] Eventually the form did become recognized as a distinct genre, and there are many American English senryū anthologies and individual senryū poet publications. One of the earliest collections (1976) of senryū published in English was *Selected Senryū* by Portland, Oregon, poet Lorraine Ellis Harr.[46] In 1987, as previously mentioned, Shūhō Ohno provided an English-language senryū-writing guide in the second part of his book, *Modern Senryu in English* and provided 224 senryū examples in English written by Japanese American poets. Dr. Ohno places an emphasis on the need for senryū to have a meaning that is clearly understood by and "echoes" sympathetically with the reader.[47] Another anthology of English senryū, *"Fig Newtons: Senryū to Go,"* was edited by Michael Dylan Welch and published in 1993.

Senryū is a recognized form in the Haiku Society of America (HSA) *Frogpond* journal and the *Modern Haiku* journal. Both journals do not separate them from haiku when publishing them, but both have contests recognizing outstanding senryū. The HSA offers this definition of senryū: "A senryū is a poem, structurally similar to haiku, that highlights the foibles of human nature, usually in a humorous or satiric way." HSA notes, "A senryū may or may not contain a season word or a grammatical break. Some Japanese senryū seem more like aphorisms, and some modern senryū in both Japanese and English avoid humor, becoming more like serious short poems in haiku form. There are also 'borderline haiku/senryū,' which may seem like one or the other, depending on how the reader interprets them."[48]

Dr. Ohno provides a humorous example of the overlap between haiku and senryū that can sometimes occur, especially if the senryū poet uses a reference to nature or animal behavior. Animal behavior is a common theme with senryū poets, as they recognize similar behaviors in humans. The example he provides is a senryū written by the senryū poet with the pen name Keisei. His senryū, focusing on the behavior of sparrows all puffy on a very cold morning, was published in Japan as a senryū. The same winter scene of puffy neckless sparrows bunched together on a bitterly cold morning in English was composed by J. W. Hackett as a haiku and submitted to the Japanese Air Lines Haiku contest in 1964. Hackett's haiku perhaps could be seen as having a focus on the season, versus the focus on the animal behavior of the senryū by Keisei. But really, when cases overlap, it is up to the author to decide what to call the poem, and it is up to the reader to interpret it.

Most of the public in the United States is unaware of the senryū genre. However, there are many poets who focus on senryū as their preferred Japanese-influenced style of poetry composition. One is Al Pizzarelli who, in a 1984 article, lamented the fact that many haiku being published at that time were really senryū and should be recognized as such.[49] Currently, the English senryū genre has many supporters. Multiple online journals exist, such as *Cattails* (they do require the poet to submit their work as either a haiku or a senryū), *Prune Juice*, and *failed haiku*. These journals provide numerous articles about senryū and publish poems online and in print. Also, online haiku educational sites promote haiku and senryū and other Japanese-influenced poetry (such as *haiga, renku*, and tanka) as social activities and assist people interested in becoming a haiku and or senryū poet. A few of these are the Haiku Society of America, Haiku Foundation, and the American Haiku Archives.

Throughout the United States and the world, numerous haiku poetry groups have formed for the sharing of haiku and senryū in English, and conferences are frequently held. The one thing all these poets do have in common is their belief that writing haiku or senryū is both challenging and entertaining and is a way to build bridges across many countries and cultures.

Shelley Baker-Gard
Portland, Oregon
2022

Timeline[1]

This timeline also includes significant historical dates for actions that adversely affected Japanese and Asian immigration to the United States, providing a historical context of the long-standing prejudices that permeate our history.

1790

On March 26, the US Congress passed the Naturalization Act, which limited citizenship to free European people. The act stipulated that any free Caucasian person, having lived in the United States for two years, was able to become a citizen.

1870

The Naturalization Act of 1870 explicitly extended the naturalization process to African Americans, who had gained citizenship rights under the Fourteenth Amendment. However, the act also explicitly denied citizenship and naturalization to Asian immigrants.

1882

The economic conditions after the Civil War and the labor movements that provoked racist fears of Chinese laborers motivated the Chinese Exclusion Act, passed in 1882 under the administration of President Chester Arthur (1829–1886). It prohibited Chinese immigration and was the first law banning immigration based on ethnicity and racial identity.[2]

1907

After the Chinese Exclusion Act was passed, the increase in Japanese immigration again became a focus of anti-Asian groups. In 1905, the Japanese and Korean Exclusion League was formed, with the intent to add Japanese and Koreans to the Chinese Exclusion Act as banned Asian groups. In 1906, when the San Francisco School Board required the segregation of the Japanese students from public schools, the Japanese government felt this was an insult to Japanese people as a whole. The Gentlemen's Agreement, an informal agreement made between

President Theodore Roosevelt and the government of Japan in 1907, eased these diplomatic tensions. The agreement stipulated that the United States would recognize the Japanese Americans residing in the United States and allow immigration of family and wives from Japan. As part of the agreement, Japan would not allow future emigration of its citizens to the United States. This agreement led to the practice of "picture brides," wherein friends and family of Japanese American bachelors would arrange for matchmaking and exchange of pictures between the prospective bride in Japan and the bachelor in the United States. The practice ended in 1920, when Japan stopped issuing passports to the picture brides. A year after the agreement, Japanese American children were allowed to attend San Francisco public schools.[3]

1924

The Immigration Act of 1924 (Johnson-Reed Act) passed on March 24. It eliminated all immigration from Asian countries (the Asian Exclusion Act was part of the 1924 Immigration Act) and stipulated immigration quotas from other countries based on the number of existing Americans with immigration ties to those countries, as indicated in the 1890 census. The sponsors of the Immigration Act were the Republican US senator from Pennsylvania, David Reed, and Albert Johnson, the Republican US representative from Washington. Johnson was supported by the local Ku Klux Clan for his anti-immigration sentiments especially directed at Jewish people, Southern and Eastern Europeans, and Chinese and Japanese immigrants.[4] These sentiments did not disappear and again became apparent when World War II started.

1941

On December 7, 1941, Pearl Harbor was attacked by the Japanese air force. Franklin D. Roosevelt approved Proclamation No. 2525, which provided for the search and confinement of people suspected of disloyalty to the United States. During December, Japanese Americans in the United States had their bank accounts frozen and businesses closed, and were forbidden to own guns, shortwave radios, and cameras. The proclamation also applied to a small number of Italian Americans and German American citizens.

1942

JANUARY: Effective January 1, 1942, all travel was frozen for Japanese residents. In January, Japanese Americans living in the western states were required to be registered and were fired from government jobs. On January 29, strategic areas of defense along the western coast and part of Arizona were determined, and people with enemy ancestry (primarily Japanese Americans) suffered forced removal from the areas.

FEBRUARY: On February 11, 1942, President Roosevelt signed Executive Order No. 9066, which paved the way for the forced removal, led by Lt. Gen. DeWitt.

MARCH: On March 11, 1942, Lt. Gen. DeWitt established the Wartime Civil Control Administration (WCCA) and named Col. Karl R. Bendetsen as the director for implementation of the plan for incarceration of the Japanese Americans living in the strategic areas. On March 18, President Roosevelt signed Executive Order No. 9102 that established the War Relocation Authority (WRA), which was to provide aid to people who were to be imprisoned. In March, curfews were invoked for all aliens and Japanese Americans. In California and Washington, the first groups of Japanese Americans were required to report to temporary detention centers known as "assembly centers," most of which were formerly stockyards. They were given only five days to pack their belongs for their incarceration at the detention centers.[5] On March 27, Japanese Americans were forbidden by the WCCA to voluntarily move to nonstrategic areas in the United States.

APRIL: Further imprisonments occurred in Washington, Oregon, and California, to the temporary detention centers.

MAY: The detention centers were established as military areas, and all the Japanese Americans residing in them were forbidden to leave by the Western Defense Command Order No. 1.

On May 19, 1942, at the North Portland WCCA Assembly Center, a newsletter was created by George Sugai, called *Evacuazette*. One thousand copies of the second edition were distributed or mailed. On May 22, the first prisoners arrived from eastern Oregon. On May 26, 250 Japanese Americans from Oregon and Washington left for incarceration at Tule Lake camp in Northern California.

JUNE: Tule Lake received groups of Japanese from rural Oregon and Washington who had not been in the temporary detention centers.

JULY: Incarceration continued at all camps. Mitsuye Endo, a US citizen, seeks a writ of habeas corpus, filed by James Purcell on her behalf, for the release of Endo and her family from the Tule Lake concentration camp. The writ stated Endo was a law-abiding loyal citizen and there were no charges made against her, yet she was being held against her will at the detention center. Her lawsuit, *Ex parte Mitsuye Endo*, eventually prevailed

The staff of the *Evacuazette*; Yuji Hiromura, editor-in-chief, is shown standing second from left. Other staff members are Ted Tsubai, managing editor; Taka Ichikawa, news editor; Chiseo Shoji, art editor; George Hijiya, sports editor; Umeko Matsubu, women's editor; and Tom Okazaki, business manager. War Relocation Authority photographs were carefully controlled to perpetuate positive public opinion about the incarceration of Japanese Americans. Photo credit: Oregon Journal Collection, Oregon Historical Society 49758.

on December 18, 1944, when the US Supreme Court ruled that the US government could not detain citizens who were loyal to the United States, and that it was an example of an "unconstitutional resort to racial discrimination." The ruling was cross-referenced to the *Korematsu v. United States*, 323 U.S. 214 (1944), which also was decided on December 18, 1944. In that ruling, Korematsu's case failed, and the exclusion orders were upheld. Two other cases also failed at the Supreme Court, *Hirabayashi v. United States*, 320 U.S. 81 (1943) and *Yasui v. United States*, 320 U.S. 115 (1943); in both of these cases, the curfew laws were upheld.[6]

AUGUST: The forced removal of more than 110,000 people, predominantly with ancestry from Japan, to temporary detention centers or directly to camps was completed as announced by the western defense commander on August 7, 1942. On August 10, the Minidoka camp in Idaho received its first group to be incarcerated.[7]

NOVEMBER: By November 3, all Japanese Americans in the military exclusion zones had been transported from temporary detention centers to the various incarceration camps in the United States.[8]

Japanese Americans outside the Pacific International Livestock Exposition building in north Portland, renamed the North Portland Assembly Center. Photo credit: Oregon Historical Society; https://www.oregonhistoryproject.org/articles/historical-records/japanese-evacuees-portland-assembly-center/#.Yul0u-zMKWY

1943

JANUARY–FEBRUARY: An all-volunteer Japanese American combat force was established by Secretary of War Henry L. Stimson. Registration for military service was based on answers from the Loyalty Questionnaire that men over age seventeen filled out while living at the assembly centers and concentration camps, including Minidoka. More than one thousand young Japanese American men volunteered from the camps to enlist.[9]

JUNE: The Supreme Court ruled against plaintiffs in *Hirabayashi v. United States* and *Yasui v. United States*. The plaintiffs challenged the legality of a curfew based solely on ethnicity. The court ruled that Executive Order No. 9066 was legal, as was Public Law 77-503 passed by Congress, which allowed for the curfew and eventual forced removal of Japanese Americans living in the western states, including citizens born in the United States. Minoru Yasui was a Portland attorney who purposely defied the curfew for Japanese Americans to provide a test case to the US Supreme Court challenging its legality. He told District Court Judge Alger Fee "every American has the right to walk up and down the streets as a freeman." Judge Fee found him guilty, asserting he had given up his citizenship because he had worked for the Japanese consulate in Chicago. He spent nine months in solitary confinement before being reimprisoned at the Minidoka, Idaho, camp. The case was then appealed to the US Supreme Court.[10]

1944

JUNE 6: D-DAY—allied forces begin invasion of France (the Japanese American regiment was sent to Italy in May).

DECEMBER 17–18: The West Coast exclusion orders that had been issued to remove the Japanese Americans from their homes were revoked, with an effective date of January 2, 1945. This allowed for the eventual return of those imprisoned to the west coast areas. On December 18, it was announced that the US military WRA camps would be closed by the end of 1945. Also on December 18, the US Supreme Court ruled against *Korematsu v. United States,* stating that the US government could legally exclude citizens based on ancestry from military areas. However, at the same time, the Supreme Court also ruled that loyal Japanese Americans could not be detained in the camps.[11]

1945

MAY 8: Germany surrenders. The week before, the Japanese American 522nd Field Battalion freed the Jewish, Romani, and other prisoners at the Dachau Nazi death camp.[12]

AUGUST 6 AND AUGUST 9: The United States dropped atomic bombs on the Japanese cities of Hiroshima and Nagasaki killing more than two hundred thousand civilians. Japan surrendered to the allies on August 15, 1945.[13]

OCTOBER–DECEMBER: All WRA incarceration camps are closed except for Tule Lake camp in Northern California, which was closed in March 1946, and the Crystal City camp in Texas, which was closed in October 1946.[14]

1948

On July 2, the Japanese American Claims Act passed, allowing Japanese Americans who had been incarcerated to file claims against the US government for property loss or damage caused by their imprisonment. Only $31 million was paid out through these claims, less than 10 percent of the estimated actual loss for the many families and individuals affected.[15]

1952

The Immigration and Nationality Act of 1952 (McCarran-Walter Act)[16] eliminated race as a basis for naturalization, and within the next decade more than forty thousand Issei were granted citizenship. However, while the act removed the banning of immigration from Asian countries, it also set a low quota of only one hundred Asian immigrants per country, excepting Japan, which had a quota that allowed 185 people per year to immigrate.

1965

The Immigration and Nationality Act of 1965 (Hart-Celler Act) removed the quota system based on ethnicity under the Lyndon B. Johnson administration. The quotas were replaced with preferential treatment given to immigrants with family in the United States, as well as the consideration of the US labor needs.

1976

On February 19, President Gerald Ford officially voided Executive Order No. 9066, thirty-four years after President Franklin D. Roosevelt had issued it to allow for the incarceration of Japanese Americans.[17]

1983

June 23: The report from the Commission on Wartime Relocation and Internment of Civilians was issued. The research concluded that the removal and/or incarceration of primarily Japanese Americans along the west coast was not a military necessity, but was motivated by racism, hysteria following the bombing of Pearl Harbor, and erroneous decision making by government and military leaders.[18]

November: Judge Marilyn Hall Patel, of the Ninth US Circuit Court in San Francisco, reversed the 1942 conviction of Fred Korematsu and ruled that his incarceration for not complying with the "evacuation order" of 1942 was not justified. The reversal was due to a writ of *coram nobis* petition filed by legal historian Peter Irons. Korematsu spoke at the hearing, and Judge Hall Patel stated that "national security must not be used to protect governmental actions from close scrutiny and accountability."[19]

1988

AUGUST 10: The US Congress passed HR 442, which acknowledged the error of the imprisonment of the Japanese Americans during World War II. It was signed by President Ronald Reagan and provided an apology, in addition to reparation payments of $20,000 to any living Japanese American who had been incarcerated. In 1989, President George Bush signed Public Law 101-162 that funded the reparation payments. The first nine payments were provided on October 9, 1990, at a ceremony in Washington, DC.[20]

2015

NOVEMBER: Minoru Yasui was posthumously awarded the Presidential Medal of Freedom by President Barack Obama.[21]

2016

The Oregon State Legislature passed a statute designating March 28 as Minoru Yasui Day, commemorating the March 28, 1942, date when Yasui walked the streets of Portland after the military curfew imposed on the Japanese residing in the west coast restricted zone.[22]

2018

JUNE 26: The Supreme Court upheld, by a vote of five to four, President Donald Trump's power to control immigration and his ban on travel from several Muslim countries, but at the same time, the court overruled the *Korematsu v. United States* conviction. Chief Justice John Roberts stated, "The forcible relocation of U.S. citizens to concentration camps based on solely on race is objectively unlawful." However, in the dissent, Justice Sonia Sotomayor warned that the court was sanctioning once again a discriminatory policy toward a "disfavored group" because of an unsubstantiated threat to national security, using the same logic the 1944 Supreme Court justices had used in the original Korematsu decision.[23]

2020

JULY 15: Tung Yin, a law professor at the Lewis and Clark Law School in Portland, Oregon, suggests a school in Portland be renamed for Minoru Yasui, for his heroism in challenging the constitutionality of Executive Order No. 9066, which enabled the incarceration of Japanese American US citizens during World War II based on race.[24]

2021

MARCH 2: Dr. Seuss Enterprises, the company that holds the rights to Dr. Seuss publications, announced that six Dr. Seuss books would no longer be published because they contained racist and insensitive imagery. The company noted that these books "portray people in ways that are hurtful and wrong." During World War II, Theodor Seuss Geisel drew racist cartoons of Japanese Americans that reflected public opinion at the time.[25]

During World War II, Dr. Seuss (Theodor Seuss Geisel) drew political cartoons. This one in particular reflected the racist viewpoints levied on the Japanese Americans at the time. Photo credit: University of San Diego Seuss Collection; uscd.edu./speccoll/pm/

Also in 2021, many incidents of racist slurs and attacks against Asian Americans were reported throughout the country during the Covid-19 virus pandemic, which was reported as having originated in China. Additionally, it should be noted, there was an increase in racially motivated attacks toward other minorities in 2021.

MAY 25: US congressional representative Grace Meng introduced bill HR 3525 to establish a national museum dedicated to Asian American and Pacific Islander American history. As of April 25, 2022, the bill was still pending approval of the House of Representatives.[26]

2022

OCTOBER 30: The editor of the *Oregonian,* Therese Bottomly, published a lengthy apology for the racist activities it supported through news articles and opinion pieces from the time it was established in 1850. This apology includes the opinion pieces it wrote during World War II, which supported the incarceration of the Japanese Americans on the west coast.[27]

Notes

Notes on Terminology

1 Neil Nakadate, *Looking after Minidoka: An American Memoir* (Bloomington: Indiana University Press, 2013), 213.

Introduction

1 Louis Fiset, "Medical Care in Camp," *Densho Encyclopedia*, https://encyclope-dia.densho.org/Medical_care_in_camp/, updated October 5, 2020.

2 Ian Barker, "Context Is Everything," *Simpler Is Better*, January 15, 2009, https://simplerisbetter.wordpress.com/2009/01/15/context-is-everything.

3 Shig Sakamoto, "Portland (Detention Facility)," *Densho Encyclopedia*, http://encyclopedia.densho.org/Portland%20%28detention%20facility%29/, updated August 13, 2021.

4 *Evacuazette*, June 23, 1942, p. 1.

5 San Francisco State University, "Japanese American Internment Curriculum: Minoru Yasui," https://web.archive.org/web/20161127084901/http://online.sfsu.edu/jaintern/yasui_bio.html, accessed March 24, 2022.

6 Minoru Yasui, "Testimony Submitted for the CWRIC hearing in Washington, D.C., July 14, 1981," https://encyclopedia.densho.org/sources/en-denshopd-i67-00333-1/, accessed September 21, 2020.

7 *Evacuazette*, July 21, 1942, pp. 3, 5; July 31, 1942, p. 2.

8 George Katagiri, "Japanese Americans in Oregon," *Oregon Encyclopedia*, https://oregonencyclopedia.org/articles/japanese_americans_in_or-egon_immigrants_from_the_west/, updated January 26, 2021.

9 Kathy Tucker, "Japanese Evacuee Tops Sugar Beets," *Oregon History Project*, https://oregonhistoryproject.org/articles/historical-records/japanese-evacuee-tops-sugar-beets/, updated 2021.

10 Allen W. Austin, "National Japanese American Student Relocation Council," *Densho Encyclopedia*, https://encyclopedia.densho.org/National%20Japanese%20American%20Student%20Relocation%20Council, updated October 8, 2020; see also Austin, *From Concentration Camp to Campus: Japanese American Students and World War II* (Urbana: University of Illinois Press, 2004).

11 Franklin Odo, "100th Infantry Battalion," *Densho Encyclopedia*, https://encyclopedia.densho.org/100th%20Infantry%20Battalion, updated October 16, 2020; see also Masayo Duus, *Unlikely Liberators: The Men of the 100th and the 442nd* (Honolulu: University of Hawai'i Press, 1987); and James M.

McCaffrey, *Going for Broke: Japanese American Soldiers in the War against Nazi Germany* (Norman: University of Oklahoma Press, 2013).

12 Jiro Nakano and Kay Nakano, eds. and trans., *Poets Behind Barbed Wire* (Honolulu: Bamboo Ridge Press, 1983), 14, 39.

13 Shizue Iwatsuki, Poem 15, trans. Stephen Kohl, in *Turning Shadows into Light: Art and Culture of the Northwest's Early Asian/Pacific Community*, ed. Mayumi Tsutakawa and Alan Chong Lau (Seattle: Young Pine Press, 1982), 63.

14 Violet Kazue de Cristoforo, ed. and trans., *May Sky: There Is Always Tomorrow: An Anthology of Japanese American Concentration Camp Kaiko Haiku* (Los Angeles: Sun and Moon Press, 1997), 283–286.

15 Violet Kazue de Cristoforo, *Ino Hana: Poetic Reflections of the Tule Lake Internment Camp* (Berkeley: University of California Bancroft Library, 1987).

16 de Cristoforo, *May Sky*, 18.

17 de Cristoforo, *May Sky*, 109.

18 Jacqueline Pearce, ed., with Michiko Kihira and Jean-Pierre Antonio, trans., "Haiku in Tashme," *British Columbia History Journal* 53, no. 1 (2020): 1.

19 Kaneko Tohta, trans. Kon Nichi Translation Group, *Haiku as Life: A Kaneko Tohta Omnibus* (Winchester, VA: Red Moon Press, 2011).

20 Teruko Kumei, "A Record of Life and a Poem of Sentiments: Japanese Immigrant Senryu, 1929–1945," *Amerikastudien / American Studies* 51, no. 1 (2006): 29–49, https://www.jstor.org/stable/41158196.

21 Makoto Ueda, *Light Verse from the Floating World: An Anthology of Premodern Senryu* (New York: Columbia University Press, 1983), 5.

22 Ueda, *Light Verse*, 3.

23 Ueda, *Light Verse*, 5.

24 Ueda, *Light Verse*, 5.

25 Ueda, *Light Verse*, 6; Lee Gurga, *Haiku: A Poet's Guide* (Lincoln, IL: Modern Haiku Press, 2003), 132.

26 William Higginson and Penny Harter, *The Haiku Handbook* (New York: Kodansha America, 1985), 20–24.

27 Gurga, *Haiku*, 133–136.

28 Hioaki Sato, *On Haiku* (New York: New Directions, 2018), 182.

29 de Cristoforo, *May Sky*, 23.

30 de Cristoforo, *May Sky*, 23.

31 Ueda, *Light Verse*, 6–7.

32 Ueda, *Light Verse*, 7.

33 Ueda, *Light Verse*, 7.

34 Ueda, *Light Verse*, 29.

35 Ueda, *Light Verse*, 10, 23, 25, 32.

36 Kumei, "Record of Life," 30; and John Michio Ohno, *Modern Senryu in English* (Seattle: Hokubi International, 1987), 12.

37 Ueda, *Light Verse*, 32–33.

38 Ueda, *Light Verse*, 32.

39 Ueda, *Light Verse*, 35.

40 Teruko Kumei, "Crossing the Ocean, Dreaming of America, Dreaming of Japan: Transpacific Transformation of Japanese Immigrants in Senryu Poems: 1929–1941," *Japanese Journal of American Studies* 16 (2005): 85–86 (Teruko Kumei, trans.).

41 Kumei, "Crossing the Ocean," 86.

42 Kumei, "Crossing the Ocean," 86.

43 Kumei, "Crossing the Ocean," 86.

44 Kumei, "Record of Life," 32.

45 Erika Niedowski, "Prisoners of Their Heritage," *Baltimore Sun*, December 6, 2004, https://www.baltimoresun.com/news/bal-te.camp06dec06-story.html.

46 Mayumi Tsutakawa, "Mitsuye Yamada," *Densho Encyclopedia*, https://encyclopedia.densho.org/Mitsuye%20Yamada, updated January 16, 2018.

47 Marvin K. Opler and Fukuzo Obayashi, "Senryu Poetry as Folk and Community Expression," *Journal of American Folklore* 58, no. 227 (1945).

48 Opler and Obayashi, "Senryu Poetry," 4.

49 Opler and Obayashi, "Senryu Poetry," 5.

50 Opler and Obayashi, "Senryu Poetry," 8–9.

51 Opler and Obayashi, "Senryu Poetry," 10.

52 Ueda, *Light Verse*, 35, trans.

53 Ueda, *Light Verse*, 35

54 Ito Yuki, "New Rising Haiku: The Evolution of Modern Japanese Haiku and the Haiku Persecution Incidents," Gendai Haiku, http://research.gendai-haiku.com/ito/new-rising-haiku.htm, accessed November 5, 2020.

55 Yuki, "New Rising Haiku."

56 Charlie Savage, "Korematsu, Long a Stain on the Supreme Court, Is Finally Tossed Out," *New York Times*, June 27, 2018.

57 Ohno, *Modern Senryu in English*, 5, 12.

58 Ohno, *Modern Senryu in English*, 1–8, 144–147.

59 See, for example, https://densho.org/.

About the Translations

1 George Katagiri, "Japanese Americans in Oregon," *Oregon Encyclopedia*, https://oregonencyclopedia.org/articles/japanese_americans_in_oregon_immigrants_from_the_west/, updated January 26, 2021.

2 Helen Craig McCullough, trans., *The Tale of the Heike* (Stanford, CA: Stanford University Press, 1988).

3 John Michio Ohno, *Modern Senryu in English* (Seattle: Hokubi International, 1987), 143.

Reflections on First-Person Experience in War Haiku

1 Kika Hotta, *Jinrui No Gogo* (The Afternoon of Humankind) (Nagano, Japan: Yu Shorin, 2021), 6, 12.

2 Hirai Shobin, ed., *Gendai No Haiku* (Modern Haiku) (Tokyo: Kodansha, 1993), 50.

3   Ty Hadman, *Dong Ha Haiku* (Kentfield, CA: Smythe-Waithe Press, 1982), 10.

4   Unpublished. Used with permission from the poet.

5   Shobin, *Gendai No Haiku.*

American English Senryū and Haiku

1   Yuzo Ota, *Basil Hall Chamberlain: Portrait of a Japanologist* (New York: Routledge, 2012).

2   Floyd Chueng, ed., *Sadakichi Hartmann: Collected Poems, 1886–1944* (Stroud, UK: Little Island Press, 2016), 11.

3   Sadakichi Hartmann, "The Japanese Conception of Poetry," *The Reader* 3 (1904): 5.

4   Chueng, *Sadakichi Hartmann,* 115.

5   Yone Noguchi, "A Proposal to American Poets," *The Reader* 3, no. 3 (1904): 248.

6   Masayo Duus, with Peter Duus, trans., *The Life of Isamu Noguchi: Journey without Borders,* (Princeton, NJ: Princeton University Press, 2004).

7   William Higginson and Penny Harter, *Haiku Handbook* (New York: Kodansha America, 1985), 51.

8   Ezra Pound, "A Few Don'ts by an Imagiste," *Poetry* (March 1913): 200–206, https://www.poetryfoundation.org/poetrymagazine/browse?contentId=58900.

9   Harold G. Henderson, *An Introduction to Haiku* (Garden City, NY: Doubleday, 1958), ix.

10   Lee Gurga, *Haiku: A Poet's Guide* (Lincoln, IL: Modern Haiku Press, 2003), 10.

11   Gurga, *Haiku,* vi–x.

12   R. H. Blyth, *A History of Haiku,* vol. 1 (Tokyo: Hokuseido Press, 1949), i–xiv.

13   C. Scott Littleton, *Shinto: Origins, Rituals, Festivals, Spirits, Sacred Places* (Oxford: Oxford University Press, 2002).

14   Andrew Juniper, *Wabi Sabi: The Japanese Art of Impermanence* (North Clarendon, VT: Tuttle Publishing, 2003), 49–50.

15   Jane Reichhold, *Basho: The Complete Haiku* (New York: Kodansha USA, 2013), 406.

16   Reichhold, *Basho,* 406.

17   Higginson and Harter, *Haiku Handbook,* 295.

18   Jane Reichhold, *Writing and Enjoying Haiku: A Hands-On Guide* (New York: Kodansha USA, 2002), 406–407.

19   Reichhold, *Basho,* 408.

20   Juniper, *Wabi Sabi,* 9, 74–75.

21   Juniper, *Wabi Sabi,* 9.

22   Kenneth Yasuda, *The Japanese Haiku: Its Essential Nature, History, and Possibilities in English* (Rutland, VT: Charles E. Tuttle, 1995), xv–xx.

23   Yasuda, *Japanese Haiku,* 34.

24 Yasuda, *Japanese Haiku*, 41–42.

25 Yasuda, *Japanese Haiku*, 49.

26 Yasuda, *Japanese Haiku*, 79–97.

27 Harold Stewart, *A Net of Fireflies: Haiku and Haiga* (Rutland, VT: Charles E. Tuttle, 1960), and *A Chime of Windbells: A Year of Japanese Haiku in English* (Rutland, VT: Charles E. Tuttle, 1969), 162–165.

28 A YouTube musical performance and lecture, "A Net of Fireflies: Song Cycle for Voice and Piano," which are compositions by Vincent Persichetti based on several of the haiku in the books, can be found at https://www.youtube.com/watch?v=Ct2jcVBrQXk; the pianist is Joshua Pearl, and the lecture is presented by Shelley Baker-Gard.

29 Dorothy Britton, *A Haiku Journey: Basho's Narrow Road to a Far Province* (New York: Kodansha International, 1974), 22.

30 R. H. Blyth, *A History of Haiku*, vol. 2 (Tokyo: Hokuseido Press, 1949), 350–351.

31 Gurga, *Haiku*, 16.

32 Harold G. Henderson, *Haiku in English* (New York: Charles E. Turtle, 1967), appx.

33 Henderson, *Haiku in English*, 42.

34 Machmiller, "Jewel in the Crown: How Form Deepens Meaning in English-Language Haiku," *Frogpond: The Journal of Haiku Society of America* 36, no. 2 (2002): 25–30.

35 "A Brief Guide to Concrete Poetry," Poets.org, May 5, 2004, https://poets.org/text/brief-guide-concrete-poetry.

36 Cor Van den Heuvel, *the window washer's pail* (*New York: Chant Press*, 1963), 11, https://www.thehaikufoundation.org/omeka/items/show/103.

37 Henderson, *Haiku in English*, 29.

38 "Definitions of Haiku and Related Terms: Report of the Definitions Committee," Haiku Society of America, September 18, 2004, https://www.hsa-haiku.org/hsa-definitions.html.

39 "Definitions of Haiku and Related Terms," https://www.hsa-haiku.org/hsa-definitions.html.

40 "Submissions Guidelines and Policies," *Modern Haiku*, http://www.modern-haiku.org/submissions.html, accessed November 18, 2020.

41 "Matsuyama Declaration," Haikupedia, https://haikupedia.org/article-haikupedia/matsuyama-declaration/, updated May 28, 2022.

42 "Matsuyama Declaration," Haikupedia.

43 Kacian, "Characteristics of American Haiku," *Frogpond* 39, no. 3 (2016): 52–55.

44 "Matsuyama Declaration," Haikupedia, no. 6.

45 Higginson and Harter, *Haiku Handbook*, 232.

46 Lorraine Ellis Harr, *Selected Senryu* (Kanona, NY: J & C Transcripts, 1976); https://thehaikufoundation.org/omeka/items/show/3846.

47 John Michio Ohno, *Modern Senryu in English* (Seattle: Hokubi International, 1987), 143.

48 "Definitions of Haiku and Related Terms," https://www.hsa-haiku.org/hsa-definitions.html, accessed November 17, 2022.

49 Al Pizzarelli, "Modern Senryū," *Simply Haiku* 3, no. 2 (Summer 2005), http://www.simplyhaiku.com/SHv3n2/reprints/Pizzarelli_modSenryū.html.

Timeline

1 The timeline was gathered from multiple sources, including the *Densho Encyclopedia* timeline (https://encyclopedia.densho.org/timeline/); the ImmigrationHistory.org timeline (https://immigrationhistory.org/timeline); a 2010 poetry exhibit by Teruko Kumei titled *Land of Joy and Sorrow: Japanese Pioneers in the Yakima Valley*, Yakima Valley Museum, https://www.yvmuseum.org/land-of-joy-and-sorrow; and Marian L. Smith, "Race, Nationality, and Reality: INS Administration of Racial Provisions in U.S. Immigration and Nationality Law Since 1898," *Prologue* 34, no. 2 (Summer 2002), https://www.archives.gov/publications/prologue/2002/summer/immigration-law-1.html.

2 See Erika Lee, *At America's Gates: Chinese Immigration during the Exclusion Era, 1882–1943* (Chapel Hill: University of North Carolina Press, 2003); and Beth Lew-Williams, *The Chinese Must Go: Violence, Exclusion, and the Making of the Alien in America* (Cambridge, MA: Harvard University Press, 2018).

3 Shiho Imai, "Gentlemen's Agreement," *Densho Encyclopedia*, https://encyclopedia.densho.org/Gentlemen's_Agreement, updated November 27, 2019.

4 Roger Snider, Brian Barnes, and Aaron Goings, *The Red Coast: Radicalism and Anti-Radicalism in Southwest Washington* (Corvallis: Oregon State University Press, 2019), 14.

5 Lauren Kessler, *Stubborn Twig: Three Generations in the Life of a Japanese American Family* (Corvallis: Oregon State University Press, 2005), 162.

6 Greg Robinson, "Ex parte Mitsuye Endo (1944)," *Densho Encyclopedia*, https://encyclopedia.densho.org/Ex_parte_Mitsuye_Endo_(1944)/, updated July 15, 2020; see also Roger Daniels, *The Japanese American Cases: The Rule of Law in Time of War* (Lawrence: University Press of Kansas, 2013).

7 Lawson Fusao Inada, ed., *Only What We Could Carry: The Japanese American Internment Experience* (Berkeley: Heyday Books, 2000), 415.

8 Inada, *Only What We Could Carry*.

9 Brian Niiya, "Japanese Americans in Military during World War II," *Densho Encyclopedia*, https://encyclopedia.densho.org/Japanese_Americans_in_military_during_World_War_II/, updated January 25, 2021; Franklin Odo, "442nd Regimental Combat Team," *Densho Encyclopedia*, https://encyclopedia.densho.org/442nd_Regimental_Combat_Team, updated October 16, 2020.

10 Kessler, *Stubborn Twig*, 166–168.

11 Robinson, "Ex parte Mitsuye Endo (1944)"; Shiho Imai, "Korematsu v. United States," *Densho Encyclopedia*, https://encyclopedia.densho.org/Korematsu%20v.%20United%20States/, updated July 29, 2020.

12 Odo, "442nd Regimental Combat Team"; see also James M. McCaffrey, *Going for Broke: Japanese American Soldiers in the War against Nazi Germany* (Norman: University of Oklahoma Press, 2013).

13 "Hiroshima and Nagasaki Bombing Timeline," Atomic Heritage Foundation, April 26, 2016, https://www.atomicheritage.org/history/hiroshima-and-nagasaki-bombing-timeline.

14 Inada, *Only What We Could Carry*, 416–417.

15 Inada, *Only What We Could Carry*, 416–417.

16 Jane Hong, "Immigration Act of 1952," *Densho Encyclopedia*, https://encyclopedia.densho.org/Immigration_Act_of_1952, updated July 7, 2020.

17 Inada, *Only What We Could Carry*, 415.

18 Sharon Yamato, "Commission on Wartime Relocation and Internment of Civilians," *Densho Encyclopedia*, https://encyclopedia.densho.org/Commission_on_Wartime_Relocation_and_Internment_of_Civilians, updated July 8, 2020.

19 Shiho Imai, "Fred Korematsu," *Densho Encyclopedia*, https://encyclopedia.densho.org/Fred%20Korematsu, updated July 15, 2020.

20 Sharon Yamato, "Civil Liberties Act of 1988," *Densho Encyclopedia*, https://encyclopedia.densho.org/Civil_Liberties_Act_of_1988/, updated August 24, 2020.

21 Peggy Nagae, "Minoru Yasui," *Oregon Encyclopedia*, https://www.oregonencyclopedia.org/articles/yasui_minoru_1916_1986_/#.Y4vW2n3MJ_8, updated November 3, 2022.

22 Nagae, "Minoru Yasui."

23 Charlie Savage, "Korematsu, Long a Stain on the Supreme Court, Is Finally Tossed Out," *New York Times,* June 27, 2018.

24 Tung Yin, "Opinion: Rename a Portland School for the deserving Minoru Yasui," *Oregonian,* July 15, 2020, https://www.oregonlive.com/opinion/2020/07/opinion-rename-a-portland-school-for-the-deserving-minoru-yasui.html.

25 Bill Chappell, "Dr. Seuss Enterprises Will Shelve 6 Books, Citing 'Hurtful' Portrayals," NPR, March 2, 2021, https://www.npr.org/2021/03/02/972777841/dr-seuss-enterprises-will-shelve-6-books-citing-hurtful-portrayals.

26 US Congress, HR 3525, May 25, 2021, https://meng.house.gov/sites/meng.house.gov/files/MENG_AAPI_Museum_Study%20Bill.pdf.

27 Therese Bottomly, ed., "Publishing Prejudice: The Oregonian's Racist Legacy," *Oregonian,* Special Section, October 30, 2022, p. 3.

About the Poets

1 Paula Johnson Burke, "The Story Locked in a Stone," *Seattle Review of Books*, November 1, 2017, https://seattlereviewofbooks.com/notes/2017/11/01/the-story-locked-in-a-stone/.

2 Vincent Wixon, "Lawson Fusao Inada (1938–)," *Oregon Encyclopedia*, July 15, 2019, https://www.oregonencyclopedia.org/articles/inada_lawson_fusao_1938_.

3 Linda Tamura, "Shizue Iwatsuki (1897–1984)," *Oregon Encyclopedia*, July 13, 2021, https://www.oregonencyclopedia.org/articles/iwatsuki_shizue_1897_1984_.

4 Tsutakawa and Chong Lau, *Turning Shadows into Light*, 63.

5 Record #700841, [Japanese-American Internee Data File], 1942–1946, Record Group 210: Records of the War Relocation Authority, 1941–1989, National Archives, Textual Archives Services Division—Archives I, Washington, DC, https://aad.archives.gov/aad/display-partial-records.jsp?f=624&mtch=1&q=700841&cat=all&dt=3099&tf=F.

6 Gail Kinsey Hill, "Hisako Saito, A Japanese American Poet Who Spanned the Cultures, Dies," *Oregonian*, March 30, 2002, B01.

7 Kumei, personal communication with the editors, June 20, 2020.

8 Kumei, personal communication with the editors, June 20, 2020.

9 *Utah Nippo*, July 1, 1942, p. 4, https://newspapers.lib.utah.edu/ark:/87278/s6z64jqt/23061644.

Bibliography

Atomic Heritage Foundation. "Hiroshima and Nagasaki Bombing Timeline." April 26, 2016. https://www.atomicheritage.org/history/hiroshima-and-nagasaki-bombing-timeline.

Austin, Allen W. *From Concentration Camp to Campus: Japanese American Students and World War II.* Urbana: University of Illinois Press, 2004.

Austin, Allen W. "National Japanese American Student Relocation Council." *Densho Encyclopedia.* https://encyclopedia.densho.org/National%20Japanese%20American%20Student%20Relocation%20Council. Last updated October 8, 2020.

Azuma, Eiichiro. "A History of Oregon's Issei, 1890–1952." *Oregon Historical Quarterly* 94, no. 4 (1993): 315–367.

Barker, Ian. "Context Is Everything." *Simpler Is Better,* January 15, 2009. https://simplerisbetter.wordpress.com/2009/01/15/context-is-everything.

Blyth, R. H. *Edo Satirical Verse Anthologies.* Tokyo: Hokuseido Press, 1961; "Edo Satirical Verse Anthologies." Haiku Foundation Digital Library. https://thehaikufoundation.org/omeka/items/show/219. Accessed November 17, 2022.

Blyth, R. H. *Haiku.* Volume 1. Tokyo: Hokuseido Press, 1949.

Blyth, R. H. *A History of Haiku.* Volume 2. Tokyo: Hokuseido Press, 1949.

Blyth, R. H. *Japanese Life and Character in Senryu.* Tokyo: Hokuseido Press, 1961.

Blyth, R. H. *Senryu.* Tokyo: Hokuseido Press, 1971; "Senryu." Haiku Foundation Digital Library. https://thehaikufoundation.org/omeka/items/show/226. Accessed November 17, 2022.

Bottomly, Therese. "Publishing Prejudice: The Oregonian's Racist Legacy." *Oregonian,* Special Section, October 30, 2022, pp. 1–3.

Britton, Dorothy. *A Haiku Journey: Basho's Narrow Road to a Far Province.* New York: Kodansha International, 1974.

Burke, Paula Johnson. "The Story Locked in a Stone." *Seattle Review of Books,* November 1, 2017. https://seattlereviewofbooks.com/notes/2017/11/01/the-story-locked-in-a-stone/.

Chamberlain, Basil Hall. "Basho and the Japanese Poetical Epigram." *Transactions of the Asiatic Society of Japan* 2 (1902): 30.

Chamberlain, Basil Hall. *Japanese Poetry.* London: John Murray, 1911.

Chappell, Bill. "Dr. Seuss Enterprises Will Shelve 6 Books, Citing 'Hurtful' Portrayals." NPR, March 2, 2021. https://www.npr.org/2021/03/02/972777841/dr-seuss-enterprises-will-shelve-6-books-citing-hurtful-portrayals.

Chueng, Floyd, ed. *Sadakichi Hartmann: Collected Poems, 1886–1944*. Stroud, UK: Little Island Press, 2016.

Chula, Margaret. *What Remains: Japanese Americana in Internment Camps, a Collection of Poetry by Margaret Chula with Art Quilts by Cathy Erickson*. Portland, OR: Katsura Press, 2009.

Collisson, Craig. "Japanese American Wartime Incarceration in Oregon." *Oregon Encyclopedia*. https://www.oregonencyclopedia.org/articles/japanese_internment/. Last updated July 27, 2022.

Daniels, Roger. *The Japanese American Cases: The Rule of Law in Time of War*. Lawrence: University Press of Kansas, 2013.

de Cristoforo, Violet Kazue. *Ino Hana: Poetic Reflections of the Tule Lake Internment Camp*. Santa Clara, CA: Self-published, 1987. Available at the University of California Berkeley Bancroft Library Northern Regional Library Facility, pf PS3554.E25 .P64; also https://oac.cdlib.org/ark:/28722/bk0016z4p62/?brand=oac4.

de Cristoforo, Violet Kazue. *May Sky: There Is Always Tomorrow: An Anthology of Japanese American Concentration Camp Kaiko Haiku*. Los Angeles: Sun and Moon Press, 1997.

Densho. *The Japanese American Legacy Project*. http://densho.org/. Accessed May 1, 2021.

Densho Encyclopedia. "Timeline." https://encyclopedia.densho.org/timeline.

Duus, Masayo. Trans. Peter Duus. *The Life of Isamu Noguchi: Journey without Borders*. Princeton, NJ: Princeton University Press, 2004.

Duus, Masayo. Trans. Peter Duus. *Unlikely Liberators: The Men of the 100th and the 442nd*. Honolulu: University of Hawai'i Press, 1987.

Evacuazette. "WCCA Newsletter: Portland, Ore." May 19–August 25, 1942. Portland: Oregon Historical Society Archives.

Failed Haiku: A Journal of English Senryu. https://failedhaiku.com. Accessed November 26, 2020.

Fiset, Louis. "Medical Care in Camp." *Densho Encyclopedia*. https://encyclopedia.densho.org/Medical_care_in_camp/. Last updated October 5, 2020.

Gold, Eric. "Within Makeshift Walls: Portland Expo Center's Era as a Prison for Japanese Americans." *Oregon Humanities* (Fall/Winter 2016). http://oregonhumanities.org/rll/magazine/might-fall-winter-2016/within-makeshift-walls/.

Gurga, Lee. *Haiku: A Poet's Guide*. Lincoln, IL: Modern Haiku Press, 2003.

Hadman, Ty. *Dong Ha Haiku*. Kentfield, CA: Smythe-Waithe Press, 1982.

Haiku Society of America. "Definitions of Haiku and Related Terms: Report of the Definitions Committee." Haiku Society of America. September 18, 2004. https://www.hsa-haiku.org/hsa-definitions.html.

Haikupedia. "Matsuyama Declaration." https://haikupedia.org/article-haikupedia/matsuyama-declaration/. Last updated May 28, 2022.

Hartmann, Sadakichi. "The Japanese Conception of Poetry." *The Reader* 3 (1904).

Hass, Robert. *The Essential Haiku, Versions of Basho, Buson and Issa*. Hopewell, NJ: The Ecco Press, 1994.

Henderson, Harold G. *Haiku in English*. New York: Charles E. Tuttle, 1967.

Henderson, Harold G. *An Introduction to Haiku: An Anthology of Poems and Poets from Basho to Shiki*. Garden City, NY: Doubleday, 1958.

Higginson, William, and Penny Harter. *The Haiku Handbook*. New York: Kodansha America, 1985.

Hill, Gail Kinsey. "Hisako Saito, a Japanese American Poet Who Spanned the Cultures, Dies." *Oregonian*, March 30, 2002, B01.

Hong, Jane. "Immigration Act of 1952." *Densho Encyclopedia*. https://encyclopedia.densho.org/Immigration_Act_of_1952. Last updated July 7, 2020.

Hotta, Kika. *Jinrui No Gogo* (The Afternoon of Humankind). Nagano, Japan: Yu Shorin, 2021.

Hyatt-Evenson, Tania. "We're Going to Wyoming and Idaho." *Oregon History Project* 2004. https://www.oregonhistoryproject.org/articles/historical-records/we39re-going-to-wyoming-amp-idaho/#.Y3bN_MfMJPY. Updated 2021; accessed November 17, 2022.

Imai, Shiho. "Fred Korematsu." *Densho Encyclopedia*. https://encyclopedia.densho.org/Fred%20Korematsu. Last updated July 15, 2020.

Imai, Shiho. "Gentlemen's Agreement." *Densho Encyclopedia*. https://encyclopedia.densho.org/Gentlemen's_Agreement. Last updated November 27, 2019.

Imai, Shiho. "Korematsu v. United States." *Densho Encyclopedia*. https://encyclopedia.densho.org/Korematsu%20v.%20United%20States. Last updated July 29, 2020.

ImmigrationHistory.org. "Timeline." https://immigrationhistory.org/timeline.

Inada, Lawson Fusao. *Legends from Camp*. Minneapolis: Coffee House Press, 1993.

Inada, Lawson Fusao. *Only What We Could Carry: The Japanese American Internment Experience*. Berkeley, CA: Heyday Books, 2000.

Juniper, Andrew. *Wabi Sabi: The Japanese Art of Impermanence*. North Clarendon, VT: Tuttle Publishing, 2003.

Kacian, Jim. "Characteristics of American Haiku." *Frogpond: The Journal of the Haiku Society of America* 39, no. 3 (2016).

Katagiri, George. "Japanese Americans in Oregon." *Oregon Encyclopedia*. https:///oregonencyclopedia.or/articles/japanese americans in oregon immigrants from the west. Last updated January 26, 2021.

Keene, Donald. *Japanese Literature*. Wisdom of the East Series. Tokyo: Tuttle Company, 1956.

Kessler, Lauren. *Stubborn Twig: Three Generations in the Life of a Japanese American Family*. Corvallis: Oregon State University Press, 2005.

Kumei, Teruko. "Crossing the Ocean, Dreaming of America, Dreaming of Japan: Transpacific Transformation of Japanese Immigrants in Senryu Poems, 1929–1941." *Japanese Journal of American Studies* 16 (2005): 81–110.

Kumei, Teruko. "A Record of Life and a Poem of Sentiments: Japanese Immigrant Senryu, 1929–1945." *Amerikastudien / American Studies* 51, no. 1 (2006): 29–49. www.jstor.org/stable/41158196.

Lee, Erika. *At America's Gates: Chinese Immigration during the Exclusion Era, 1882–1943*. Chapel Hill: University of North Carolina Press, 2003.

Lew-Williams, Beth. *The Chinese Must Go: Violence, Exclusion, and the Making of the Alien in America*. Cambridge, MA: Harvard University Press, 2018.

Littleton, C. Scott. *Shinto: Origins, Rituals, Festivals, Spirits, Sacred Places*. Oxford: Oxford University Press, 2002.

Machmiller, Patricia J. "Jewel in the Crown: How Form Deepens Meaning in English-Language Haiku." *Frogpond: The Journal of the Haiku Society of America* 36, no. 2 (2002): 25–30.

Matsuda Gruenewald, Mary. *Looking Like the Enemy, My Story of Imprisonment in Japanese-American Internment Camps*. Troutdale, OR: New Sage Press, 2005.

McCaffrey, James M. *Going for Broke: Japanese American Soldiers in the War against Nazi Germany*. Norman: University of Oklahoma Press, 2013.

McCullough, Helen Craig, trans. *The Tale of the Heike*. Stanford, CA: Stanford University Press, 1988.

Modern Haiku. "Submissions Guidelines and Policies." https://www.modern-haiku.org/submissions.html. Accessed November 18, 2020.

Nagae, Peggy. "Minoru Yasui." *Oregon Encyclopedia*. https://oregonencyclopedia.org/articles/yasui minoru 1916 1986_/. Last updated March 24, 2022.

Nakadate, Neil. *Looking after Minidoka: An American Memoir*. Bloomington: Indiana University Press, 2013.

Nakano, Jiro, and Kay Nakano, eds. and trans. *Poets behind Barbed Wire*. Honolulu, HI: Bamboo Ridge Press, 1983.

National Archives. WRA records of Japanese Americans Incarcerated. https://aad.archives.gov/aad/. Accessed June 23, 2022.

Neidowski, Erika. "Prisoners of Their Heritage." *Baltimore Sun*, December 6, 2004. https://www.baltimoresun.com/news/bal-te.camp06dec06-story.html.

Niiya, Brian. "Japanese Americans in Military during World War II." *Densho Encyclopedia*. https://encyclopedia.densho.org/Japanese_Americans_in_military_during_World_War_I. Last updated January 25, 2021.

Noguchi, Yone. "A Proposal to American Poets." *The Reader* 3, no. 3 (1904): 248.

Noguchi, Yone. *The Spirit of Japanese Poetry*. London: John Murray, 1914.

Odo, Franklin. "442nd Regimental Combat Team." *Densho Encyclopedia*. https://encyclopedia.densho.org/442nd_Regimental_Combat_Team. Last updated October 16, 2020.

Odo, Franklin. "100th Infantry Battalion." *Densho Encyclopedia*. https://encyclopedia.densho.org/100th%20Infantry%20Battalion. Last updated October 16, 2020.

Ohno, John Michio. *Modern Senryu in English*. Seattle: Hokubi International, 1987.

Opler, Marvin K., and Fukuzo Obayashi. "Senryu Poetry as Folk and Community Expression." *Journal of American Folklore* 58, no. 227 (1945): 1–11.

Oppenheim, Joanne. *Dear Miss Breed: True Stories of the Japanese American Incarceration during World War II and a Librarian Who Made a Difference*. New York: Scholastic, 2006.

Oregon Humanities. "Portland Expo Center: A Hidden History." Video, 6:21. 2017. http://oregonhumanities.org/rll/beyond-the-margins/portland-expo-center-hidden-history/.

Ota, Yuzo. *Basil Hall Chamberlain: Portrait of a Japanologist*. New York: Routledge, 2012.

Pearce, Jacqueline, and Jean-Pierre Antonio. "Haiku in Tashme: The Legacy of Sukeo 'Sam' Sameshima." *British Columbia History Journal* 53, no. 1 (2020): 5–12.

Pizzarelli, Al. "Modern Senryu." *Simply Haiku* 3, no. 2 (Summer 2005). http://www.simplyhaiku.com/SHv3n2/reprints/Pizzarelli_modSenryū.html.

Poets.org. "A Brief Guide to Concrete Poetry." May 5, 2004. https://poets.org/text/brief-guide-concrete-poetry.

Pound, Ezra. "A Few Don'ts by an Imagiste." *Poetry*, March 1913, pp. 200–206. https://www.poetryfoundation.org/poetrymagazine/browse?contentId=58900.

Prune Juice. https://prunejuice.wordpress.com/about/. Accessed November 26, 2020.

Reeves, Richard. *Infamy: The Shocking Story of the Japanese American Internment in World War II*. New York: Henry Holt and Company, 2015.

Reichhold, Jane. *Basho: The Complete Haiku*. New York: Kodansha USA, 2013.

Reichhold, Jane. *Writing and Enjoying Haiku: A Hands-On Guide*. New York: Kodansha USA, 2002.

Robinson, Greg. "Ex parte Mitsuye Endo (1944)." *Densho Encyclopedia*. https://encyclopedia.densho.org/Ex_parte_Mitsuye_Endo_(1944)/. Last updated July 15, 2020.

Rosenow, Ce. "Written in the Face of Adversity: The Senryu Tradition in America." *Literary Imagination* 12, no. 2 (2010): 210–213.

Russel, Jan Jarboe. *The Train to Crystal City*. New York: Scribner, Simon and Schuster, 2016.

Sakamoto, Henry Shig. "Portland (Detention Facility)." *Densho Encyclopedia*. https://encyclopedia.densho.org/Prtland%20%28detention%20facility%29/. Last updated August 13, 2021.

San Francisco State University. "Japanese American Internment Curriculum: Minoru Yasui." https://web.archive.org/web/20161127084901/https://online.sfsu.edu/jaintern/yasui bio.html.

Sato, Hioaki. *On Haiku*. New York: New Directions, 2018.

Savage, Charlie. "Korematsu, Long a Stain on the Supreme Court, Is Finally Tossed Out." *New York Times*, June 27, 2018.

Shobin, Hirai, ed. *Gendai No Haiku* (Modern Haiku). Tokyo: Kodansha, 1993.

Smith, Marian L. "Race, Nationality, and Reality: INS Administration of Racial Provisions in U.S. Immigration and Nationality Law Since 1898." *Prologue* 34, no. 2 (Summer 2002). https://www.archives.gov/publications/prologue/2002/summer/immigration-law-1.html.

Snider, Roger, Brian Barnes, and Aaron Goings. *The Red Coast: Radicalism and Anti-Radicalism in Southwest Washington*. Corvallis: Oregon State University Press, 2019.

Sone, Monica. *Nisei Daughter*. Seattle: University of Washington Press, 1979.

Stewart, Harold. *A Chime of Windbells: A Year of Japanese Haiku in English.* Rutland, VT: Charles E. Tuttle, 1969.

Stewart, Harold. *A Net of Fireflies: Haiku and Haiga.* Rutland, VT: Charles E. Tuttle, 1960.

Tamura, Linda. "Shizue Iwatsuki (1897–1984)." *Oregon Encyclopedia.* July 13, 2021. https://www.oregonencyclopedia.org/articles/ iwatsuki_shizue_1897_1984_.

Tohta, Kaneko. *Haiku as Life: A Kaneko Tohta Omnibus: Essays, an Interview, Commentaries and Haiku in Translation by the Kon Nichi Teanslation Group (Richard Gilbert Masahiro Hori, Ito Yuki, Dvis Ostman, Koun Franz, Trancy Franz, Kanamitsu Takayoshi).* Winchester, VA: Red Moon Press, 2011.

Tsutakawa, Mayumi. "Mitsuye Yamada." *Densho Encyclopedia.* https://encyclope-dia.densho.org/Mitsuye%20Yamada. Last updated January 16, 2018.

Tsutakawa, Mayumi, and Alan Chong Lau, eds. *Turning Shadows into Light: Art and Culture of the Northwest's Early Asian/Pacific Community.* Seattle: Young Pine Press, 1982.

Tucker, Kathy. "Japanese Evacuee Tops Sugar Beets." Photograph CN 021008. April 1943. *Oregon History Project.* https://oregonhistoryproject.org/articles/ historical-records/japanese-evacuee-tops-sugar-beets/.

Ueda, Makoto. *Light Verse from the Floating World: An Anthology of Premodern Senryu.* New York: Columbia University Press, 1983.

US Congress H.R. 3525, May 25, 2021. https://meng.house.gov/sites/meng. house.gov/files/MENG_AAPI_Museum_Study%20Bill.pdf.

Utah Nippo. July 1, 1942. https://newspapers.lib.utah.edu/ark:/87278/ s6z64jqt/23061644.

Van den Heuvel, Cor. *the window-washer's pail. New York: Chant Press,* 1963; Haiku Foundation Digital Library. https://www.thehaikufoundation.org/omeka/ items/show/103.

Wixon, Vincent. "Lawson Fusao Inada (1938–)." *Oregon Encyclopedia.* July 15, 2019. file:///C:/Users/User/Desktop/inada_lawson_fusao_1938_.pdf.

Yamada, Mitsuye. *Camp Notes and Other Writings.* New Brunswick, NJ: Rutgers University Press, 1992.

Yamato, Sharon. "Civil Liberties Act of 1988." *Densho Encyclopedia.* https:// encyclopedia.densho.org/Civil_Liberties_Act_of_1988/. Last updated August 24, 2020.

Yamato, Sharon. "Commission on Wartime Relocation and Internment of Civilians." *Densho Encyclopedia.* https://encyclopedia.densho.org/ Commission_on_Wartime_Relocation_and_Internment_of_Civilians. Last updated July 8, 2020.

Yasuda, Kenneth. "Haiku and Painting." *Tulean Dispatch Magazine,* March 10, 1943.

Yasuda, Kenneth. *The Japanese Haiku: Its Essential Nature, History, and Possibilities in English.* Rutland, VT: Charles E. Tuttle, 1995.

Yasui, Minoru. "Testimony Submitted for the CWRIC Hearing in Washington, D.C., July 14, 1981." *Densho Encyclopedia*. https://enclyclopedia.densho.org/sources/en-denshopd-i67-00333-1/. Accessed September 21, 2020.

Yin, Tung. "Opinion: Rename a Portland School for the Deserving Minoru Yasui." *Oregonian*, July 15, 2020. https://www.oregonlive.com/opinion/2020/07/opinion-rename-a-portland-school-for-the-deserving-minoru-yasui.html.

Yuki, Ito. *New Rising Haiku: The Evolution of Modern Japanese Haiku and the Haiku Persecution Incidents*. Winchester, VA: Red Moon Press, 2007. gendaihaiku.com.

Granite memorial rock at the Lakeview Cemetery in Seattle, inscribed with a senryū by Shinjiro Honda. Photo credit: Ian Gard, 2022

About the Poets

This section contains a few details on the of life of the poets, who are listed in alphabetical order. The editors often ran into dead ends looking for biographical information on them, partly because they used pen names. Much appreciation goes to Professor Teruko Kumei for her help in finding information on the poets' actual names in Japanese and English and the areas they were from. Since the journal of the senryū was kept by Masaki Kinoshita and was saved by his family, his biographical notes are the most extensive.

HONDA, SHINJIRO (KAHŌ) 本多しんじろう (華芳)
(senryū no. 66)
Shinjiro Honda was born in 1877 and came to the United States in 1905. He lived in various cities in Washington including Yakima and Wapato. He married a Japanese Issei woman, and they had one child, Teresa Yoshi Honda. His wife died in 1930.

During the 1930s, Honda was an influential leader in the Japanese senryū community in Washington. He was the editor of the first anthology of Japanese senryū in the United States, *Hokubei Senryū,* published in 1935 by the Hokubei Senryū Gosenkai group. This group was active in Yakima and still meets (as of 2018) in Tacoma, with a membership of Japanese women who arrived after World War II.

Honda and his daughter were both incarcerated in the Portland Assembly Center and later were moved to the Heart Mountain Center in Wyoming. Shinjiro Honda died two days after arriving, from esophageal cancer. After the war, his body was sent to his daughter, who arranged for a traditional Buddhist cremation. At the Lakeview Cemetery in Seattle, a granite memorial rock is inscribed with a senryū by Honda:

> To live! That is good . . .
> But to die, released from care—
> Is that not good too?[1]

Masaki Kinoshita

KINOSHITA, MASAKI (JŌNAN) 木下まさき (城南) (senryū nos. 1, 2, 4, 5, 7, 8, 9, 10, 11, 12, 13, 14, 15, 16, 18, 19, 20, 21, 23, 25, 28, 31, 32, 34, 35, 36, 37, 38, 39, 40, 41, 43, 44, 45, 46, 47, 48, 49, 52, 53, 55, 57, 59, 60, 61, 62, 63)

(*Masaki Kinoshita biography by Duane Watari*)

1896—Born in Kumamoto, Kyushu, Japan

1915—Immigrated to the United States to work and better himself and his family. Japan was struggling economically to support many of its citizens.

1915 to 1927—Worked doing various general labor jobs in Portland, Hood River, Seattle, and Central Washington.

1927 to 1940—Built and opened first business on rented property, since non-US citizens were not able to own property. Purchased property in 1940 by putting the name of his daughter, who was a US citizen, on the deed.

1942—Because of the executive order by President Roosevelt following the declaration of war with Japan, his family was mandated to report to the WCCA Assembly Center in North Portland (former animal stock yard) within forty-eight hours of notice. The family of five was given a ten-foot-by-twelve-foot area to live in, with no ceiling or door, only the existing stall walls or partitions, amid the smell of animal waste and flies.

1942 to 1945—Incarcerated at the Minidoka, Idaho, concentration camp, behind barbed wire with a constant twenty-four-hour military guard watch. His family endured extremely cold winters and very hot summers but survived until all the imprisoned were released in early 1945. He returned to Portland to restart the family business. When Masaki Kinoshita was at the assembly center, he joined the Bara Ginsha (City of Roses) group.

Post-1945

- Remained active in the Bara Ginsha Senryū group and served as the treasurer and the *komon* (honorary adviser) for more than twenty-seven years.
- Recipient of several local awards for his contribution to an informal alliance of Japanese American businesses.
- In 1979, he was the recipient of an award (see image) from the Japanese emperor for his dedication to preserving Japanese culture in the United States and for his contributions to the cultural understanding between Americans and Japanese.
- Continued to work at his family business in the Alberta neighborhood of Portland until finally retiring in the late 1970s.

Masaki Kinoshita continued to write senryū until he died in 1997 at the age of ninety-nine in Portland, Oregon. One of his senryū is engraved on a large display rock at the Japanese American Historical Plaza in Portland.

Masaki Kinoshita's certificate of award from the Japanese emperor for his dedication to preserving Japanese culture in the United States.

IKO, KYOKUO (USON) 伊香きょくお（芋 村）(senryū no. 30)
Kyokuo Iko was born in Japan in 1888; he came to the United States when he was twenty-two years old, after changing his original aspiration to become a Buddhist priest in Japan. Once in the United States, he became a farmer in Washington. After leaving the Portland Assembly Center, Iko and his family were moved to the Heart Mountain camp in Wyoming. There he began watercolor painting and used scenes from the surroundings of Heart Mountain as his inspiration. His artwork was displayed at the Cody, Wyoming, Buffalo Bill Historical Center (now the Buffalo Bill Center of the West) in 2014.

INADA, LAWSON FUSAO いなだふさお (poetry engraved on granite stones at the Portland Japanese Memorial Plaza)
Lawson Fusao Inada was born in Fresno, California, in 1938 to Nisei parents. His mother was a teacher and his father a dentist. His Issei grandparents established a fish market in Fresno after they emigrated from Japan. During World War II, the Inada family was incarcerated at the Pinedale Assembly Center in Fresno, transferred to the Jerome Arkansas camp, and then moved to the Amache Camp in Colorado. Fortunately, their German and Italian friends were able to take care of things while the Inadas were away from their home and businesses.

Inada obtained his master of fine arts degree from the University of Oregon and taught at Southern Oregon University for many years. He has published multiple works of nonfiction and poetry, including the American Book Award winner *Legends from Camp*, written in 1992, from which his son Miles created an animated video in 2004; and *Drawing the Line* (1997), which won the Oregon Book Award. Both of these books' poems are steeped in the experience of the incarceration of the Japanese Americans during World War II. He is also coeditor of the comprehensive reference work, *Only What We Could Carry: The Japanese Internment Experience* (2000). In 2006, Governor Ted Kulongoski appointed Lawson Fusao Inada the fifth Oregon poet laureate. Currently, Inada and his wife Janet reside in Oregon, and he continues to write wise words for all to learn from.[2]

IWATSUKI, SHIZUE いわつきしずえ (tanka engraved on granite stones at the Portland Japanese Memorial Plaza)
Shizue Iwatsuki was an Issei born in 1897 in Japan; she died in Hood River, Oregon, in 1984. She immigrated to the United States in 1916. With her husband Kamegoro, they farmed an apple orchard in Hood

River. In 1942, they were sent to the Pinedale Assembly Center in Fresno, California. She wrote tanka poetry and organized several Japanese American women's groups in the Hood River area before and after World War II. In 1974, Emperor Hirohito of Japan acknowledged her as an outstanding poet, and she was presented with the Sixth Class Order of the Precious Crown award for her leadership in many organizations and cultural endeavors. She was named Woman of the Year by the City of Hood River in 1974, and today visitors can see one of her tanka on a stone column at the History Museum of Hood River County.[3] The following is a tanka she wrote while incarcerated at Minidoka:

> Deeply moved
> By wretched scenes
> Of camp life,
> My heart mourns[4]

KIDO, GEORGE (HISATARO) きど (久太郎) (senryū no. 3)

George Kido is registered in the National Archives WRA database as being born in Japan in 1896 and coming to the United States in 1914. He worked as a truck farmer in Oregon and was incarcerated at Minidoka. Many members of the Kido family moved to Ontario, Oregon, and Idaho after the war. No obituary has been found in either Oregon or Idaho.

KUROKAWA, KAORU (KENTSUKU) 黒川かおる (剣突) (senryū nos. 54 and 65)

Kurokawa was born in Japan in 1882 and came to the United States in 1903, where he worked as a farm laborer in Yakima, Washington. After leaving the Portland Assembly Center, he was incarcerated at the Heart Mountain Camp in Wyoming. No obituary was found.

MAKINO, SHIZUKO (CHOUBOU) 牧野てい一郎 or しずこ (丁坊) (senryū no. 51)

The biographical research did not provide a clear picture of this poet's first name. However, the most likely possible match is Shizuko Makino, who, according to the WRA records, was born in 1900 in southern Japan. She came to the United States in 1920 and lived in Clackamas, Oregon. She spoke Japanese and worked as a sales clerk and as a seamstress. She was a widow at the time of her incarceration at Minidoka. There are many senryū by Shizuko Makino published in the book by Shūhō (John Michio) Ohno, *Modern Senryu in English*.

MIHARA, SHIGERU (GOICHI)[5] みはらしげる (吾以知)
(senryū nos. 33, 42, 56)
Shigeru Mihara was born in 1890 on Shikoku Island, Japan, to parents both born in Japan. He resided in Yakima County, Washington, and reported to the Portland Assembly Center for the initial incarceration. He was later incarcerated at the Heart Mountain Camp in Wyoming.

MIZOGUCHI, AINASUKE (HIKARI) 溝口あいなすけ (ひかり)
(senryū no. 27)
Ainasuke Mizoguchi was born in southern Japan in 1889 and immigrated in 1905 with his parents to the United States. He lived in Oregon and worked in the restaurant and hotel business at the time of his incarceration. No other biographical information was found.

SAITO, HISAKO (RYŪKO) 斉藤ひさこ (龍子) (senryū no. 6, and
senryū on the Japanese American Historical Plaza Memorial Stone).
<Hisako Saito was born in Portland, Oregon, in 1913, but because of childhood illnesses she lived for twenty years in Japan. When she returned to Portland in 1936, her father had found a husband for her, Kane Saito, and they settled in Globe, Oregon, where she began writing senryū. She

Hisako Saito. Photo originally appeared in *Touching the Stones: Tracing One Hundred Years of Japanese History*, Mark Sherman and George Katagiri, eds., Oregon Nikkei Endowment, 1994. Photo credit: George Kozawa

was a prominent senryū poet in Portland and a leader of the Bara Ginsha Senryū group. She was also the editor of their senryū journal.

In 1987, she was awarded by the Japanese government and the emperor the Order of the Precious Crown, Ripple, a high honor given for support of Japanese American relations. Saito also served on the boards of the Nikkei Endowment and the Oregon Nikkei Legacy Center. She helped found the center, an organization dedicated to preserving the history of Japanese Americans, and she participated in the center's opening in the spring of 1998.[6] One of her poems appears on a granite memorial stone at the Japanese American Historical Plaza in Portland.

SHIMIZU, KATSUHIKO (SHOUSUI) 清水かつひこ (勝水)
(senryū nos. 24 and 29)
Katsuhiko Shimizu was born in Shingu-shi, Wakayama, Japan, in 1895 and came to the United State in 1913. He lived in Yakima, Washington, with his wife before the war and worked as a farmer. Some of his prewar senryū are in Teruko Kumei's personal senryū archives.[7] After the war he went to Chicago and changed his penname (*gago*) to 頑突 (Gantsuku).

SUENAGA, TARO (SEN TARO) すえなが太郎 (仙太郎)
(senryū no. 67)
Taro Suenaga was born in 1888 in Japan and arrived in the United States in 1912. He spent most of his time in the state of Washington, working as a farm manager. He was incarcerated at the Heart Mountain camp. After World War II, he continued to write senryū. Several of his poems appear in the book by Shūhō (John Michio) Ono, *Modern Senryu in English*.

TAMURA, TOYOKO[8] (SHINSETSU) 田村とよこ (深雪)
(senryū no. 50)
ToyokoTamura was born in 1899 in Shizuoka Japan. She came to the United States in 1921. She was one of the active senryū poets living in Oregon prior to World War II. She and her husband were incarcerated at Minidoka. No other biographical information was found.

TOMORI, MASAKO (MOKUGYO) 登森まさこ (木魚)
(senryū nos. 26 and 64)
Masako Tomori, according to the National Archives (WRA records) database, was born in Japan in 1913. Arriving in the United States around 1924, she lived in Oregon prior to World War II. She and her husband Mokuo and their two children were incarcerated at Minidoka. Many of

Masako's senryū were published in the book by Shūhō (John Michio) Ohno, *Modern Senryu in English*.

TSUYUKI, SHOHEI (ROSHYOU) 露木昌平 (露昌)
(senryū nos. 17 and 58)
Shouhei Tsuyuki was born in Japan in 1884 and immigrated to the United States in 1908. He lived in Wapato, Washington, with his wife and was a farm laborer. They were incarcerated at the Heart Mountain center.

YOKOTA, ROY (SOUU) 横田 (草雨) (senryū no. 22)
Mr. Roy Yokota was born in Oregon in 1907 to Japanese immigrants and died in 1969. He was incarcerated with his two-year-old son, Stephen Yokota, at the Portland Assembly Center. His wife, Sigeko Yokota, was trained in nursing and was sent to the assembly center in Puyallup, Washington. While incarcerated at Minidoka, he sent a senryū to the Japanese American newspaper *Yuta Nippo* for publication (published in Salt Lake City, Utah, from 1914 to 1991).[9] His family was sent to Caldwell, Idaho, to work as farm laborers. His second son was born in 1944 in Ontario, Oregon. The family moved back to the Milwaukie, Oregon, area sometime after the war. He was a longtime member of the Bara Ginsha Senryū group in Portland.

About the Editors

SHELLEY BAKER-GARD, BS, MS

Shelley Baker-Gard is the current Haiku Society of America (HSA) coordinator for Oregon. She has been writing English haiku and senryū for many years and has been published in several anthologies, including *New Bridges: A Haiku Anthology* (Portland Haiku Group, 2018); *Ribbons*; and *Frogpond*, the HSA journal. She is a Portland State University graduate, with a BS in anthropology and an MS in communications. For many years, Shelley worked as a process manager and project manager at telecommunication corporations. She was born in Portland, Oregon, where she continues to live with her family. Her favorite pastime is to write haiku based on her experiences with nature while digging in the garden, and traveling along the Springwater Corridor Trail in Portland.

MICHAEL FREILING, PHD

Mike was born in San Francisco and attended University of San Francisco as an undergraduate, where he first became interested in poetry through the works of Allen Ginsberg, Gary Snyder, and other poets of the Beat Generation. As a grad student at MIT, Mike found the time to study poetry under David Ferry at Wellesley and was a cofounder and contributor to the first issue of *Rune*, which eventually became MIT's official literary magazine (http://runemag.mit.edu/index.php).

In 1977, Mike was named a Luce Scholar (http://www.hluce.org/lsprogram.aspx), with an appointment at Kyoto University. During his scholarship year, Mike studied Japanese and produced a translation of the *Hyaku Nin Isshu*, a well-known anthology of Heian period tanka that includes poems by authors such as Lady Murasaki, Sei Shonagon, Ki no Tsurayuki, and Sugawara no Michizane.

In 2014, Mike returned to Japan for the first time in twenty-five years and began work on a series of poems that recorded his experiences at different shrines and temples around Kyoto, Tokyo, and Kanazawa. Mike's poems and translations have been published in *Seashores*, and the Writers in Kyoto annual anthologies.

In 2020, Mike founded Shimenawa no Michi, to leverage his experience as a financial analyst and investment adviser into a broader initiative to help people navigate the challenges of life, love, and the search for transcendence. Mike also holds a PhD in artificial intelligence from MIT and a chartered financial analyst (CFA) designation from the CFA Institute.

SATSUKI TAKIKAWA

Satsuki Takikawa was born and raised in Kyoto, Japan, where she still makes her home. She graduated from Sophia University in Tokyo with a degree in German literature and studied English for three and a half years in the United Kingdom before returning to Kyoto to teach English and German at Notre Dame Academy. From 2006 to 2008, she served as vice principal of the school, and as principal from 2008 to 2012. Since 2014, she has taught English at Kenmei Gakuin Academy in Sakai,  Japan. In her spare time, she enjoys woodcarving, weaving, and painting. Satsuki is the granddaughter of Yukitoki Takikawa and the daughter of Haruo Takikawa, who were both well-known in Japan for taking principled stands in favor of reason and civility against extremists on both the right and the left as deans of the law schools at Kyoto University and Osaka University, respectively.

DUANE WATARI

Duane Watari is a third-generation (Sansei) Japanese American. Born and raised in a three-generation family in Portland, Oregon, Duane still resides in the area. Married, with one daughter, he spends time with family, including his mother, who is one hundred years old and the daughter of the senryū poet Masaki Kinoshita (Jōnan). Like her family, she was also incarcerated at the Portland Assembly Center and Minidoka, Idaho. Duane remains active as well as a strong supporter in the Japanese American community.